Slice the Salami
TIPS FOR LIFE
AND
LEADERSHIP

one slice at a time

Artie Lynnworth

 INFINITY
PUBLISHING

Copyright © 2010 by Arthur Lynnworth
Original illustrations and cover art by Kate Johnson Design

ISBN 978-0-7414-6002-8

Printed in the United States of America

Published March 2013

INFINITY PUBLISHING
1094 New DeHaven Street, Suite 100
West Conshohocken, PA 19428-2713
Toll-free (877) BUY BOOK
Local Phone (610) 941-9999
Fax (610) 941-9959
Info@buybooksontheweb.com
www.buybooksontheweb.com

Dedication

This book is dedicated to my dear wife of over 40 years, Margy, for her decades of support and encouragement to me to follow my passions. She's my best friend and ally. Nearly all of the writing of this book was done at her side, as we do most of the fun things in our lives.

Contents

Slice the Salami

Tips for life and leadership, one slice at a time

Foreword

This book is about techniques for success in life and leadership, provided in bite-sized morsels, easy to savor and digest. In fact, the strange title, "Slice the Salami," is centered on the idea that you could choke on a salami if you tried to eat it whole, but a slice at a time makes great sandwiches and eventually allows you to consume the entire salami. Likewise, making changes in your life, for career leadership or at-home satisfaction, can be accomplished one step at a time.

This book is based on my 40-year career in a demanding industry, with real-life lessons learned and condensed here in short yet powerful chapters that provide concrete tips for success. The topics are easy to read, with fun and memorable examples, graphics and exercises. Yet, these themes are based on typical challenges we all face. Solutions are provided with step-by-step approaches you can implement to achieve long-term results that will pay off for you.

How do I know they will work? Because they have worked for me and for scores of professionals, friends and family members that I have coached to success. From an entry level engineering position, I had the good fortune to rise rapidly through the corporate ladder from plant manager (the youngest in my company) to senior vice president, responsible for a half-billion dollars in annual sales, plus an international assignment as general manager in Chile, South America. The techniques that enabled my recognition and reward are shared in these chapters. I have presented much of this material in corporate workshops, with my staffs as I moved from one job responsibility to another, and even at the university level, where I created, developed and taught a semester-long curriculum for business school students. The techniques work.

Read at your leisure, from cover to cover, or cherry-pick chapters that capture your interest. Try the methods for success explained here. Active participation, rather than passive reading, reinforces skills. Enjoy the benefits that follow by achieving executive presence, work-life balance, and control of your life through time management, while also making ethical choices and rejuvenating passion in what you do.

In fact, there are several chapters on how to prepare for interviews (how to take an interview, as a job applicant, or give one, as any one of the interviewers in the screening and hiring process) and how to improve your résumé, even if you have been out of the job market for a while.

In addition, many of the chapters provide techniques for non-work situations, with family or friends, including how to modify the behaviors of those who are not doing what you wish (such as children, neighbors, or maybe even your spouse), and how to relax to enjoy your life with continuous learning, a positive attitude and reduced anxiety. The object lessons from my experiences are summarized in quick-read chapters that cover the following themes:

Chapter 1 – Slice the Salami: The importance of implementing change one step at a time, gaining momentum and motivation along the way.

Chapter 2 – See the Flames, Smell the Smoke: Critical communications, and how to implement change with a sense of urgency, when you don't have time to slice the salami.

Chapter 3 – If I Only Had the Time: Time management techniques for short-term and long-term success at home and at work.

Chapter 4 – They Don't Wear Shoes: It's all about attitude.

Chapter 5 – Be a Change Maker: How to be the leader of change in your life, department, organization, family and community.

Chapter 6 – The Power of Positive Reinforcement: Behavioral techniques that work.

Chapter 7 – Continuous Learning: The importance of this practice, and how to apply it to grow and succeed.

Chapter 8 – Teamwork: A vital skill for the success of any group.

Chapter 9 – The Four-to-One Rule: How helping others will help you.

Chapter 10 – Visibility: How to be seen in constructive ways and how to make a difference where it counts.

Chapter 11 – Cross the Threshold: Getting into the supervisor's office and why.

Chapter 12 – Don't Forget: Why fail-safe follow-up (so you don't forget your commitments) is critical to success, and how to manage this skill.

I was fortunate to have worked with mentoring and model bosses, with support teams that were dedicated to results, and to have had a variety of experiences that offered many learning opportunities. Of course, I also worked with difficult people, stubborn subordinates and high-pressure challenges. This book is a digest of key leadership skills that can gain success for you, with many tips about how to anticipate and deal with potential threats to your success. Some of us learn the hard way, and some benefit from the experience of others. I wish you the best with the fastest and most productive route to your own success.

Sometimes we win, sometimes we learn. This book gives you the opportunity to learn, so that you can win!

Why should you believe anything that I say? Because what I learned and applied on and off the job, succeeded. What I taught others, allowed them to succeed. What I share here will help you to succeed. It's that simple, and it works. Let me now share some highlights of my career as background, and reinforcement that these powerful concepts are functional, easy to understand, and yield results.

My career and personal life provided a wonderful training-ground to learn a lot, with a broad range of interpersonal experiences and challenges. These work-lessons and life-lessons will serve you as well. As you will see below, I was rewarded for various successes through my career with increasing responsibility and more learning opportunities. Two outstanding companies, Allied Chemical and Occidental Chemical Corporation provided a wealth of leadership training and support during my 40 years with them (12 at Allied and 28 at OxyChem). Fortunately, the techniques for corporate success do translate to non-work situations as well, and thereby provide excellent models for your own progress, either in or away from an office, detailed throughout this book.

I began my career as an electrical engineer. After starting as a summer-student in a large chemical complex, I graduated from college the following year and began work at this same site. Who knew then that this would be the start of a four-decade career in the chemical industry? During my first three years, working during the day and going to night school, I earned my Master's degree in engineering administration, thereby gaining credibility and responsibility at work with added knowledge and credentials from my formal education. My good fortune and dedication to leadership excellence enabled steady and consistent career growth as follows:

- From entry-level engineering assignments, I rapidly progressed to department head for an industrial maintenance and construction group of several hundred employees, and then quickly to operations superintendent for a chemical processing unit. Throughout the initial years of my career, I achieved new standards for maintenance reliability and operational performance, which positioned me for promotion to plant manager and more. My early career years provided a *second education*, that is to say, a life experience beyond classrooms, textbooks and tests, which enriched my appreciation for human relations, motivation and communication. This book's chapters on time management, "Cross the Threshold" and attitude include several of the tips that bolstered my early and rapid rise in the corporation. These ideas can work for you.

- As plant manager at four different USA sites, ranging from small plants, with about 100 workers, to a large plant with over 700 at one site (including two different labor unions and a non-union workforce), I further refined my practices and performance. Recognition included receiving global corporate awards for the best Profit Improvement Program in the company (even back-to-back annual awards at two different plants, with the second award following my relocation from one site to another), as work teams were inspired to unprecedented performance. The chapters that deal with visibility, teamwork and communications, as well as creating a sense of urgency in an organization, can serve you as clear models for how to inspire similar excellence and dedication in your own group. Likewise, the leadership techniques explained in this book were the basis for my plants obtaining top global corporate awards for environmental performance and dramatic improvements in employee safety.

- When changing from manufacturing to business unit responsibility, about mid-way through my career, I served as vice president and general manager of a plastics division that, prior to my appointment, had seven consecutive years of losses. In my first year, we turned a profit, with subsequent 40% year-over-year profit growth, and regained market penetration as we recaptured customers previously discouraged by the former lackluster performance of this division. A new sense of urgency and change stimulated further business development. The first two chapters of this book address how to make changes successfully, either a step at a time or more rapidly, depending on your circumstances. Additionally, themes such as the *four-to-one rule*, for helping others, will give you more keys to unlock secrets to success.

- With subsequent promotion to senior vice president, responsible for half of my corporation's specialty chemicals group, I had a half-billion dollars of annual sales responsibility with five independent global business units across Japan, Europe, and North America. We generated one new product launch per month for over a year, negotiated a successful new joint venture with a Japanese corporation, and constructed the newest phenolic plastic molding compound plant in North America for high-tech automotive applications. Global perspectives and cultural differences thus add another dimension to the messages contained in this book. With added responsibility come added obligations for how you run your life and your business. Themes such as ethics and values as well as behavioral basics offer additional topics for your success.

- During the last decade of my career, while serving as our corporation's general manager for operations in Chile, South America, we achieved the highest profit and record sales for this business unit, obtained a respectable position in the top 20 "Best Companies to Work for in Chile," and received national safety and environmental awards. Remote independent leadership has its own set of demands, and techniques from the "Three Eyes" chapter will give you additional routes to further success.

The tips from this book apply to the personal side of life as well. It's not just about job satisfaction and growth. Topics such as communications, positive reinforcement, continuous learning, ethics and how to "Be Happy," have strengthened my relationships with family and friends. The information in the coming chapters can do the same for you.

I am fortunate to have been married for over four decades to my loving and supportive wife, Margy. I am confident that the experiences we shared and the lessons we learned together during this period, reflected in these pages, can add to your own satisfactions in life, love, hobbies and work.

Throughout this whirlwind career, my greatest satisfaction has been the development of people. Aside from having contributed to guiding the careers of hundreds of employees under my charge, before I retired, I continue to serve as a volunteer mentor, now over 15 years (at the time of this writing), with the Menttium Corporation's global program of annual mentoring partnerships (see www.Menttium.com). I've also served on their Advisory Board. In addition, I've been an expert panel member for the Human Capital Institute's focus on mentoring, which included my participation in their global web-casts. The Institute is a think-tank in Washington DC. I love to mentor and coach, and this book is another opportunity to do so.

These experiences, plus decades of team sports (New York City's Brooklyn Technical High School gymnastics team captain, Syracuse University gymnastics team captain, and assistant gymnastics coach at North Syracuse High School) provided additional opportunities for me to learn and to refine techniques of motivation, teamwork, communication and leadership. My passion to share such techniques led to the creation of this book.

I sincerely hope that you will find these chapters enlighten-ing, entertaining and rewarding. I extend to you my best wishes for your leadership success at work and your satisfaction with life in general, away from the office. Now please turn the page to start your first slice.

Enjoy!

Foreword

Artie Lynnworth

Chapter 1
Slice the Salami

Tips for life and leadership, one slice at a time

This book will help you in your life and your work, and even help you separate the two. You can start here, or jump around the book as you wish. It doesn't matter. By the end of the book, you'll have learned practical tips to save you time, enhance the joys in your life, and maybe even get you one or more promotions at work from practical tips that you can absorb as easily as your favorite sandwich. But I'm getting a little ahead of myself here.

You'll get the most out of this book when you try some new things. If all you want to do is read, save yourself some money and put this book back on the shelf. If you already bought it, sorry! I guess you will have to try stuff to get your money's worth. If you really want to learn how to do things better, smarter, faster, easier, and to get others to do the same, then keep on reading and give this a shot.

After all, what is leadership about anyway? It's about change. Leaders pull us ahead of the competition and inspire us to greatness. You can do neither by continuing with the same-old, same-old. To get the most out of life and work, to

1

lead yourself and others to excel, you have to be good at the change process, as well as a variety of other practical techniques that facilitate that process.

We'll cover these elements through stories, life lessons and a dozen exercises. Yes, you will get to try things, at least while reading the book, and then with practice on your own where it counts: at home and at work. You will learn by thinking and doing. You'll use forms and formats that can make a difference in your success and the success of those you care about: family, friends and the team that looks to you for leadership. And all of this, with just a slice at a time.

Here's one of those stories I was just talking about.

Want to lose 50 pounds fast?

When my wife, Margy, and I lived near Houston Texas, we passed by an advertising billboard that caught my attention alongside one of the city's major freeways. It had a model of a large stationary exercise bicycle built into the sign, and a giant message: "Want to lose 50 pounds fast?"

As you know, speeding along the highway there's not a lot of time to read a detailed message. I saw the ad and thought to myself (as probably thousands of others had also done), "I wonder how they can help anyone quickly lose that much weight? It must be a great exercise program." Their explanation was clear, concise and humorous. In the second part of their ad they explained: "Use our classified ads to sell your used equipment." Ah! 50 pounds of equipment, not 50 pounds of fat. This clever message probably has meaning for many of us.

The ad hit home for my wife and me, since we used to joke about one of our own stationary exercise bikes that seemed to let us burn more calories moving it from one place in the house to another rather than from our time on it doing exercise. Yet, this simple advertisement serves as a good reference for what this chapter and book is all about: how to make change in your own life, or to help others change theirs when you need them to do things differently. The need for change may be in your work environment, or in a non-work situation. Change is fundamental to progress. To be a good leader and to have satisfaction in your personal life normally involves trying new things, making changes and growing. Too often, this is easier said than done.

Like with an exercise bike, we may get excited to make drastic changes to lose weight or begin a new program, only to find days later that we fell off the wagon and returned to our old habits. Why does this happen, and how can we achieve the long-term improvements we seek? We can do it one slice at a time. Let me explain.

The normal cycle

Just as in the bicycle story, the normal cycle in most of our lives is that we become inspired about making some change. Something triggers our motivation and we say to ourselves, "Today is the first day of the rest of my life, and today I am going to make a difference!" We buy the exercise bike, all the associated paraphernalia and the *right* clothes for the workouts, and then we set up our new plan: a dedicated half hour every morning. In addition, we say to ourselves, "I may as well change my poor eating habits too, and eliminate my after dinner cookies, my between-meal snacks, and the junk food that I enjoy." Exercise, better eating habits, and a clean life style. I'm set!

How long does it last? Perhaps as long as it takes to get the first charley horse or after-workout pains and aching muscles. A few days later, the discomfort wins over inspiration and we return to our old habits. How can we break this unproductive cycle?

One bite at a time

The concept of "Slice the Salami" is simple. It applies not only to a new exercise routine for yourself, but can be as effective in changing your behavioral patterns and practices at work. The slice the salami approach can also influence others, with positive changes in a member of your family or work-team. To understand the concept, visualize the following.

If you try to eat a whole salami at one time, you may choke. It's too much. However, if you make yourself a nice sandwich, putting one or more slices of the salami between a couple pieces of your favorite bread, perhaps enhancing the snack with the best tasting mustard, and whatever else you enjoy to round-out the meal, the sandwich goes down easily. Even the thought of making the sandwich starts the salivary process going as you anticipate the tasty meal. If you're a vegetarian, the concept is still valid. Just think *soy* salami, or other non-meat equivalent, rather than be distracted by the specific ingredient. Then again, who actually knows what is really inside salami! *A slice at a time* is what's important.

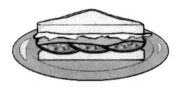

Don't choke on a salami. The sandwich goes down easily.

The next day you have another slice and another sandwich. Before you know it, you've eaten the whole salami. It's the same as the weight-loss effort: a pound at a time is what is important. Slow but sure is better than going overboard at first, getting frustrated and then quitting.

Change, a step at a time

The process of successful change depends on many factors. The prime motivation must be the desire to change. That behavioral step must then be reinforced in positive ways for us to continue making what at first may appear as a sacrifice, giving up the comfortable routines that have worked for us in the past. Doing something new or different is not always easy. However, small steps, with success, breed motivation to take another step and try some more.

With the exercise routine as an example, it's much easier to begin gradually. In my personal experience, this slow-ramp-up approach typically has a higher probability of success than going full throttle from the start. Perhaps a five or ten-minute exercise sequence gets the body and habits started, with less shock and more reward. You can notch-up the level of intensity and dedication as time goes on, as new habits take hold. Rome wasn't built in a day, and neither are life changes. How can you not afford five or ten minutes per day to try establishing a new routine that you hope will become a healthy and important new habit?

What about clutter? Slicing the salami can work the same way. Sometimes when you know you should clean up an area, such as your workspace in the office or at home in the garage or playroom, the overall task may appear overwhelming. It seems as though it is too much work to even begin, so you put it off and the piles keep growing. On the other hand, you may get inspired one day and say to yourself, "I will give this one hour per day and it will be done in a few days." Unfortunately, the second day there doesn't seem to be an hour of time available, and by the third day you have lost the momentum and spirit to attack the challenge. So the clutter remains and continues to gather.

However, if you instead committed to yourself, "I will de-clutter this area each day for only ten minutes." How can you not afford those ten minutes? The barrier to entry is small.

You can see yourself handling a short ten-minute task and then moving on. You can repeat this every day. Instead of targeting a whole-job cleanup, you instead make a reasonable and achievable goal to clean one square foot of desktop, or one corner, shelf or edge of the playroom. One bit at a time works. In a workweek, your steady yet brief dedication will generate five square feet of clear space or one wall empty of clutter. You can step back, enjoy seeing your progress, and be motivated to continue the next week with more success following.

You may gradually get inspired to dedicate more time each day to the task, improving your systems to prohibit clutter from gathering (such as creating new file folders to collect information in an orderly way, or providing new spaces for things to be stored at home). Later chapters in this book will more deeply discuss the issues of goal setting (Chapter 14), time management (Chapter 3) and behavior modification (Chapter 6), all of which will further assist you in having the time and capability to replace chaos with order. For now, let's just stick to the basics of taking small steps before we run.

This same slice the salami principle also applies to how you might approach trying to get approval from your supervisor (or spouse?) for a project or concept that needs agreement to proceed.

Great ideas!

In the work environment, many of us have great ideas. The problem is that often most of our jobs don't allow independent implementation. We need approval from our boss, or someone else to make the change happen. What do we often do in preparing to convince those with authority to approve our plan? We want to tell them that our idea is wonderful, and should be implemented *now*! But we first want to be ready when we tell them about our great idea.

Typically, we might therefore make sure that we have not jumped the gun and approached the decision maker too soon. We get all our ducks in a row, as we become even more excited that our idea has merit and can't fail. We start to imagine the end result, the praise we will get for the dramatic new approach, and we are excited to begin. The supervisor comes. We take our moment and spit-out the master plan all at once, only to be crestfallen when the shortsighted over-controlling naysayer says *"No way!"*

What went wrong? We choked the boss on the salami! When did we start to let the boss smell the salami or see the special ingredients? When did we set the stage for taking a bite? When did we activate the supervisor's salivary glands to want to taste that sandwich?

Once again, the process of change is most successful a step at a time. Of course, you need to get your ducks in a row, but the issue is one of delivery and timing. You can begin by gradually educating the boss about the need for change, and then plant the seeds for your solution. This is the part where motivation to change is created, establishing in the boss the understanding that all is not well and a solution is possible.

Perhaps begin with explaining that you have some basic ideas for solving the problem and that you'd appreciate the supervisor's feedback and expertise to help critique the possible new direction. Buy-in helps too, so getting that involvement up-front, without yet having to make the final decision, adds more success factors to the equation.

In fact, the supervisor may actually have some better ideas to complement your original thoughts and, if implemented, may even create a better result. Additionally, considering that your supervisor's ideas are part of the solution will probably increase the likelihood that he or she will accept your ultimate recommendations.

At home or with friends, the same concept applies. Perhaps you are thinking about the best way to spend your vacation time. Think salami, and share. Begin your communication process early, discussing how to relax together, offering ideas and perspectives about the benefits of your proposed vacation destination. Don't get it all planned and do a plan-dump on the other vacation participants before they have even begun to see the benefit of your proposal. Perhaps you can begin with gathering a few brochures, and request feedback, as you exchange comments to align expectations. Slice a few ideas at a time, and share them with enthusiasm.

A slow yes instead of a fast no

Sure, the sandwich process instead of the whole salami takes more time. But I'd rather have a slow yes than a fast no. In other words, I'd rather make the investment of time to cultivate an idea and ultimately get it accepted, than to force a quick decision and get it shot down now.

Once the no-go decision has been made, it often is impossible to even discuss the issue again. Keeping your idea alive with interaction, development and adjustments allows you additional chances to get what you finally are after. This steady movement in the right direction, towards your ultimate target, is the same as your steady progress to lose weight, de-clutter a work or home area, go on a fun vacation or see your steady progress in polishing off the remainder of that long salami.

This book was created to share over a dozen practical techniques for leadership success and life success. Slice the salami is just one of them. You need not read each chapter in sequence, though sometimes there are relevant links to the successive themes. The ideas are not rocket science, but rather they are simple concepts that you can grasp and use immediately for more satisfaction on your job and at home. You can gain more success with getting your ideas across and accepted, and can have fun with personal development and change.

This book is intended to be easy to digest, a short chapter at a time, a slice at a time. Read a bit, and digest it. Read some more and *try it* in your professional and personal environment. Read some more and consider how you might apply yet another technique for success. You need not choke on the whole salami, by reading the book cover to cover at one sitting. Instead, bite off as much as you enjoy to fully engage your interest and motivation.

Some of you may now be saying to yourselves that the "Slice the Salami" technique of this chapter is great if there's time, but "I can't wait forever on some issues." Perhaps you are right. Some things are best cultivated over time, and others need immediate change. For example, you may have a job that demands that you make drastic and rapid change in your group's performance to survive. You don't have the luxury to work the *sandwich process*, generating interest, involvement, and gradual buy-in over time. The *slow yes* may imply death before decision. If you can't wait, what then?

That's the theme for the next chapter: "See the Flames, Smell the Smoke!"

When you are ready for another leadership snack or life morsel, please take another bite and read on.

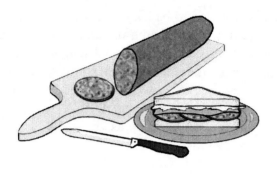

Chapter 2

See the Flames, Smell the Smoke!

Let's imagine that you have a big challenge ahead of you. You've been mandated to get your group to drastically and quickly change what they are now doing. The challenge may require restructuring your organization for a corporate-dictated headcount reduction, it may require big cuts in spending that you know are needed in order to be more competitive, or quick changes are needed because you've been told to launch a product or project with greater speed than has ever been done before at your location.

At home, it might represent the reality of a tough economy and the job loss of an income earner, with the drastic need for family members to do their share of immediate cost control. For whatever reason, you don't have the luxury to "Slice the Salami" with slow and steady progress towards your goal (see Chapter 1). You have to make change happen *now!*

These sorts of challenges might demand crisis management. The conditions indicate that urgency is needed, total commitment and unity of purpose from the responding team is essential, and the success of the task hinges on crystal clear communications. The crisis might be immediate, such as responding to an impending danger, or longer duration, such as one of the examples listed above, (restructuring, cost reductions or project launch) where the solution may extend over days, weeks or months. However, in all these cases you do not have the luxury of leisure. Decisions must be made quickly, plans set and unified action taken.

During such critical times, effective communications are vital. Likewise, teamwork is essential. We will address teamwork further in Chapter 8, but for now at least recognize that how you share the message and sense of urgency, and how you mobilize a group effort, can make the difference between success and disaster. How do you instill this sense of importance, speed, common purpose and focus for action?

Change, Focus, Speed!

I had a boss once who had worked for the international company BASF. They used a slogan "Change, Focus, Speed!" to internally get the concept across to all their employees that change is needed for continuous improvement, attention to the task at hand is critical, and that this all must be done as quickly as possible. Speed was a key element to the process.

On the other hand, I've had engineers explain to me that there are three variables to any task, speed-quality-cost, that constrain your levels of freedom to make things happen. You can pick any two of the variables, but not all three.

For example, you can have something quick and with high quality, but then cannot expect it to be cheap. Or, you can have it cheap and fast, but then the quality will suffer. Or, you can have it with great quality and low cost, but don't plan for it to be done quickly. Accordingly, if speed is your priority, be aware that this emphasis may impact other characteristics of your project (such as cost or quality), and thus must be taken into account as you plan the right strategy for your purposes.

Your role as a leader and change maker at work or at home is to combine the challenges of *change-focus-speed* with the reality of constraints, *speed-quality-cost*, to get the desired result. The key question is often "How do I get the people to understand that this is critical to our survival, and that they have to help us succeed?"

The focus of this chapter addresses ways to wake-up the group, generate a sense of urgency and inspire each individual to take an active part in the problem's solution. Understanding how to share the vision, using communication techniques that work, and dismantling common obstacles to success, will enable you to meet your challenge with the power of the team.

Teaching the elephant to dance

Effective leaders can teach almost anything!

Some people have said that organizations are similar to elephants – slow to change. This topic is covered in depth in a helpful book that deals with how to be successful with the corporate change process. "Teaching the Elephant to Dance

– Empowering Change in Your Organization," by James A. Belasco, Ph.D., immediately addresses the problem in Chapter 2 of the book. Dr. Belasco writes:

> *"Remember the elephant training parable. Trainers shackle young elephants with heavy chains to deeply embedded stakes. In that way the elephant learns to stay in place. Older elephants never try to leave even though they have the strength to pull the stake and move beyond. Their conditioning limits their movement with only a small metal bracelet around their foot – attached to nothing.*
>
> *"Like powerful elephants, many companies are bound by earlier conditioning constraints. "We've always done it this way" is as limiting to an organization's progress as the unattached chain around the elephant's foot.*
>
> *"Yet when the circus tent catches on fire – and the elephant sees the flames with its own eyes and smells the smoke with its own nostrils – it forgets its old conditioning and changes. Your task: set a fire so your people see the flames with their own eyes and smell the smoke with their own nostrils – without burning the tent down. And anyone can set the fire at any level in the organization."*

Learn how to *set the fire* with inspirational leadership in a way that becomes personal to each member of your group, your work-team or family, so each of them sees the flames and smells the smoke. That's the point of this chapter.

Getting your message across

How do you let people understand the problem and get fired-up to help with the solution? Although you have a clear picture of the situation that needs changing, you need to find the ways to communicate the problem and engage your group to discover possible solutions and implement improvements.

To better understand how, let's take a few moments to discuss communication basics, recognize the different tools that we can use, and then sharpen the message to hit home and make the challenge personal. In addition, we will look at one common pitfall, the feeling that one person's effort will never make a difference, and see how to attack this potential obstacle.

Communication basics

We want to get our message understood by another person or a group of individuals. We can view the process of getting the message across as part of a communication system, which consists of a source, signal, receiver, channel of communication and filters. There's also a feedback loop, which allows us to evaluate the strength of the signal at the receiver so that we can then make adjustments, as needed, to improve the reception of the signal.

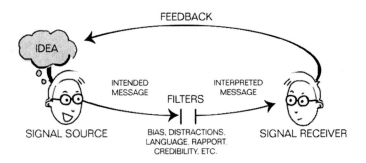

A communication system

Put simply, we (the source) have a signal (the message) that we want someone to get (the receiver) with as much clarity as possible. We can select from a variety of options to send the message, such as email, telephone, face-to-face or many other ways (the communication channels). Between the recipient and us are various elements that can obscure the message (filters). Finally, we try to interpret how well the message is received (through feedback) and work to improve the re-transmission of the message itself (follow-up with a clarifying statement).

That probably sounds somewhat technical, similar to an electrical engineer explaining how your radio works, but the fundamentals of effective communication do indeed depend on assuring that we improve each part of this system in order to maximize the potential for our message to get through. If the elephant can't see the flames, because it is blind, that's a big filter that prevents motivation to move.

Accordingly, we need to anticipate the potential filters between the receiver and ourselves and select the best channels of communication possible. Also, our message itself, the signal, should be clear, crisp and easily understood. We can be saying all the right words, but if they are in the wrong language, the recipient is as good as deaf.

Messages, memos and mimes

Pick your communication channel. Some are better than others, and by selecting the best method for your purpose you improve your odds for success.

During a university course where I taught students about career preparation and effective communications techniques, we discussed channels of communication. We listed various options, such as the written memo, a telephone, books, TV, videos, PowerPoint, etc. Then I asked the students to rank what they thought were generally the least effective and the most effective channels to use for message transmission. An expected list began to develop, indicating that face-to-face is generally better than a written message (although written communication may be best for highly technical or detailed instructions, such as contracts and operational procedures), when one sharp student came up with the best description I've yet heard for the poorest channel of communication possible. Can you guess what he suggested? A mime on the telephone!

Are you trying to get your message across as though you were a mime on the telephone, waving your hands, making faces, offering lots of body movement, but generating no sound? Are you being heard? Are you expending a lot of energy, but you get feedback to indicate your message has not gotten through? What can you do to improve the signal strength and reception?

First, pick the right channel. Use the best methods for delivering your message. Some studies indicate that after listening to a typical speech of 10 minutes, the average person has heard, evaluated precisely and understood only about 50% of what was said. After 48 hours, this retention has dropped another 50%, to 25% of the original content, and after a week, typically only about 10% is still retained.

In fact, in the book "Why We Want You to be Rich: Two Men – One Message," authors Donald Trump and Robert T. Kiyosaki present the "Cone of Learning." This information was based on a 1969 study to find the most effective way to learn. Their book includes a table that shows that after two weeks we tend to remember 90% of what we say and do, through active involvement tasks such as doing the real thing or simulating a real experience. This favorable topic retention would be expected if you can get your listener to do something, to have physical activity to touch, feel or handle items related to the topic. On the other hand, according to this particular study, after two weeks people only remember about 20% of what they hear and 10% of what they read, since these are passive activities, so they don't stick.

Hmm, I guess you had better do more than just read this book! You actually have to try these chapter techniques in your daily routines to retain the messages and skills beyond two weeks from now!

Regardless of the specific statistic of exactly how much is remembered in one or two weeks after only hearing or listening to something, the point is that people forget most of what they read or hear in a short time if their role has been passive. So if you are trying to communicate effectively, to motivate others to do something, how do you increase the odds that your audience (one person or a group) will remember more and take action?

Generally, your odds go up as you do things face-to-face. In addition, you will likely get better results if you can engage the other person. Involve them to *see*, and involve them to *do*. That means you should work to get your listener's active participation in the discussion, and get him or her physically involved, such as touching something, handling a document, and doing more than just sitting there while you do all the work.

Better yet, for ideal memory retention, in addition to *see* and *do*, there is also *teach*. The *"see one, do one, teach one"* model used in medical schools has great validity for improving message and skill retention. Students of medicine first see how techniques are done, and then as they advance they do them with the aid of a more experienced professor or higher-level student coaching them. Finally, the more advanced students are then asked to teach entry-level students themselves, to continue the cycle of learning. The act of preparing to teach another person and then to do the teaching helps move concepts from short-term memory to long-term memory.

As mentioned earlier, to get the most out of this book, you should try the techniques. For greater retention, share these techniques with your staff, family and friends by teaching them what you have learned. In normal communications, however, we are mostly concerned that the listener will at least understand what we are talking about and retain the message for as long afterwards as possible. As a minimum therefore, be sure to have them engage with the *see* and *do* phase of communication and learning.

For example, it often helps to begin your conversation or presentation with a question. This forces the other person to think about the issue, and form an opinion. This also gives you immediate feedback, to let you know if you and your listener are on the same wavelength.

This engaging is a two-way street. If the listener gives you feedback, you must show that you understand the response. Typically, you can accomplish this by re-stating the listener's comment in your own words (this also gives that person your feedback to confirm that his or her comment to you was properly understood). Your act of asking for feedback not only gives you confirmation that your message is being understood, but by requesting input, the listener becomes more engaged and invested in the issue. You build unity of purpose. Feedback is a critical part of the communications loop.

Your receptivity to this feedback is critical as well. You do not want to have your listener or listeners sense that you may be dismissing their input out of hand, rather than give it serious consideration. The two-way street must be open and cooperative for effective communication.

Written communication typically has less potential to motivate action than communication done in person. Also, you have no feedback. Did the recipients read your message at all, did they scowl and toss your letter in the trash, or did they become inspired by your words and change their behavior that instant? Use the best channels available, and prepare your message and delivery in advance to make best use of the time you have.

Anticipate the potential filters, and work to remove them

Between you and the recipient of your message are many potential filters. Understanding what these filters might be, and taking proactive action, through planning, to reduce or eliminate them, will further improve your chances that your message will be better understood, and thus acted upon properly.

What might be possible filters?

- Language – not only is the issue whether you are speaking English, regardless of whether your listeners have or do not have English as their first-language, but what vocabulary you use is also relevant. Is your audience a board of directors, or is it a group of blue-collar personnel? I'm not talking about intelligence (a shop mechanic may be more astute than a board member), but I'm talking about words that can be easily understood and are familiar. Talk straight and clearly for the listeners gathered.

- Rapport – do you and the listener have any connection between you, as a common bond of friendship or trust, or does the listener start with some skepticism or doubt about who you are or what you are about to deliver?

- Credibility – does the audience see you as credible? What has been your track record with this group? Can you be trusted by them? If you sense the history has been scarred, it may be better to have another person deliver the message.

- Noise – can the people hear you? As simple as this may seem, some speakers overlook the obvious: what are the conditions of the room for people to hear what you have to say, see your visual aids, and interact with you during the presentation?

- Distractions – time of day (at work is it close to lunch or quitting time, or at home is your communication when the kids are eager to watch their favorite TV show?), visual or audio (what's going on outside the window, or in the next noisy room?), or clutter at the head table can all drain attention from you and your message.

- Predisposition – does the audience already have a likely opinion on the issue? Perhaps their bias is based on incorrect data and your first role is to set the record straight.

- Other – what else might influence your listener so that he or she is not getting your message as you intend it to be received?

How about boredom? This surprising filter is discussed in "Don't be Such a Scientist: Talking Substance in an Age of Style," by Randy Olson (Copyright © 2009 Randy Olson. Reproduced by permission of Island Press, Washington, D.C.). This is a book geared to teach scientists how to communicate more effectively with a non-scientific audience. Dr. Olson states:

"It's about stimulation. Something that is interesting stimulates the neurons in the brain. Something that's boring doesn't. And when the brain is numbed into disinterest, communication doesn't take place."

He also states:

"...communication is not just one element in the struggle to make science relevant. It is *the* central element. Because if you gather scientific knowledge but are unable to convey it to others in a correct and compelling form, you might as well not even have bothered to gather the information."

By thinking ahead about your audience, and the possible filters to your message, you can construct a communications plan that works to offset these obstructions to an otherwise clear message. Preparation pays.

New challenges to communication

Around 2010, the concept of "Results Only Workplace Environment" (ROWE) was getting popular news coverage. These ROWEs are locations where offsite work and flexible hours are permitted, or even encouraged, rather than the traditional 9 to 5 in-office mandates. Employees now may spend all of their day working from home, and the output of their work, the results, is what counts, instead of their appearance of working by being in the office all day long. One human resource manager talked about the problem of "presenteeism" (as opposed to absenteeism) at work, which she says is when people are present physically, but their mind is elsewhere, or in her words, "they are not *really* there." Productive work from home is far superior to at-work presence without productivity.

Telecommuting is another term that is used for at-home work through computers. You can find dozens of job opportunities on the Internet when you search "telecommuting." Accordingly, telecommuting and ROWEs focus on the employee's actual contribution, regardless of their physical location. However, this means that there are fewer opportunities for at-work face-to-face contacts, onsite brainstorming to solve problems, or the chance to visit with the supervisor to discuss ideas and proposals in person. As a result, this filter of distance must be included in a pre-communication plan to assure that your message gets through as effectively as possible, despite your inability to look your listener in the eyes as you speak to him or her.

As an aside, as a volunteer mentor for the Menttium Corporation, my last decade of activity has been in their virtual program. This means that my mentees have been in distant places such as Mexico, Brazil and Argentina as well as spread across the USA. Our monthly conversations have been by telephone, email and Skype. As in telecommuting and ROWEs, this distance creates new challenges for communications. A modern leader or manager must develop the necessary skills to enable effective dialogue regardless of distance and communication channels.

Make it personal

Another technique to consider for improving communication effectiveness and message clarity is to make the message understandable to the audience on a personal level. Find analogies that relate to the audience. If you are trying to explain how the company's costs have gone up drastically, consider using the household budget as an example.

People can better relate to the cost of gas at the filling station, the cost of a bus or train in their city, or to the household electric or phone bill, than to the mega-bucks that a large corporation has to manage. If, as an example, you speak about their teenager's use of the cell phone driving up the family's monthly phone bill by 100%, that is perhaps better understood first, before talking about a parts supplier's price hike. After sharing the concept of increased phone bills, you can then proceed with a presentation that shows the relation of your company's parts supply costs to the changes that have occurred. With this personal touch technique, you can improve the odds that your audience will grasp the impact of the message.

Similarly, the same *personalization* of the issues that are effective during a presentation at work can apply as well for an at-home situation. If a family crisis demands that all participants share in control of costs, you can enhance the communication with a personal connection.

Building up a family budget, and showing the bills (actually having the kids read and touch the papers that come from utility companies, so that they engage physically with the issue), is a start to understanding how the parts of a household budget are structured. However, this impersonal data needs to become personal. A similar accounting of the child's personal expenses and available funds, that is to say the allowance, can better communicate the issue and solution needed. Understanding the relationship between resource limitations (allowance) and expenses (the things they want to buy or do), generates the foundation for understanding priorities, sacrifices and planning required to support the family's escape from crisis.

What can I do?

Unfortunately, many people listen, but then say to themselves, "What can I do? Why bother? One person's action will never change this condition."

I am often reminded of the quote attributed to Margaret Mead (1901-1978), the famous anthropologist:

"Never think that the efforts of one dedicated individual can not change the course of history. Indeed, it is the only thing that ever has."

Your role, as leader and communicator, is to capture the understanding of each individual, with effective channels of communication, and personal examples each of them can relate to, in order to allow each person to see the flames and smell the smoke. Then help these individuals to understand that the solution of the problem will come from the combined total of each person's individual commitment to action.

Do the math – the power of one

I've often done the math with my organizations. You can begin by asking something such as: "Can you come up with a simple idea that will save the company at least $10?" I explain that it doesn't have to be rocket science. It doesn't have to be drastic. It can be a simple elimination of some outdated form that wastes our time every day.

With this example of eliminating a useless form as a start, I can show my team that we save on paper, we save on time, and we save on all the downstream efforts to handle, read, and file this obsolete document. A little brainstorming will likely generate several $10 ideas. Then do the math. If each smart person (that's everybody in our organization!) simply generates one new idea per day, times over 200 working days a year, times the number of persons we have in our organization, we save $X dollars per year. And that's for only a simple idea that will save the company $10. You each do make a difference! Together we can change our world and put out the fire that could destroy us.

Think before you speak

This is obvious, but worth mentioning: think before you speak. We have all probably said something, and just as the words were leaving our mouth we thought, "I wish I hadn't said that!"

During routine conversations, and especially during critical communications, the words we use and the way we deliver them are vital to our successful transmission of our message. As the stakes get higher, where urgency or survival hang on the spoken word, think first. Do you need to create a sense of calm and orderliness despite the chaos surrounding you? Do you need to create a sense of crisis despite the apathy surrounding you? Are your words and your body language giving a consistent message? Does your tone of voice reinforce what you want to say or does it distract?

The front-end of the communication process begins with your intent (your internal thought of the message) and your way to express that issue. Aside from how you engage the listener, and your choice of vocabulary, consider your overall delivery and the particular way to express yourself in the context of the situation. If you begin with a poor message, and sub-par delivery, it only gets worse as it travels through the various downstream filters and obstacles. We've all seen the expression, "Be sure brain is engaged before putting mouth into gear." Good advice.

You can do it!

Understanding the communications channel, picking the best medium for communications, anticipating and knocking down potential filters, engaging your listeners and soliciting feedback to assure your message is being transmitted as clearly as possible, keeping the attention of your audience through questions and interaction, making the message understood through at-home examples and simple language, letting people understand how they can make a difference, and helping them to see the flames and smell the smoke all contribute to increasing your odds for successful change-making that has a sense of urgency. You can create change *now*, and accomplish it with the power of your team.

Whether your need for change is urgent (getting your team to sense the urgency of an issue and to take action, in other words to see the flames and smell the smoke), or you have the luxury to implement slower incremental changes (slicing the salami), we all are typically challenged by deadlines and time constraints. The better we can manage our time for the short-term or long-term, the more successful we can be. That's the topic for Chapter 3, time management. Please read on. Have another bite of the salami.

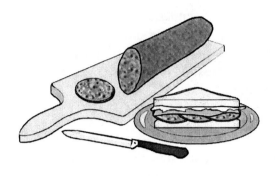

Chapter 3

If I Only Had the Time

Time is a circus always packing up and moving away.......Ben Hecht

Living is entirely too time-consuming.......Irene Petere

Procrastination: the art of keeping up with yesterday.......Don Marquis

Tick-tock, tick-tock, tick-tock

60..., 60..., 24..., 7..., 52. Sixty seconds in a minute, sixty minutes in an hour, twenty four hours in a day, seven days in a week, fifty two weeks in a year, and how many years in a task, career or lifetime? More importantly, how do you make use of that time? Does it manage you, or do you manage your time?

Getting control of time, with simple yet productive time management techniques, is the focus of this chapter. Understanding these techniques and applying them to your daily routines can make a great difference in your personal and career success, your satisfaction with life and your balance between things you have to do and things you want to do. Let time be a tool that works for you, not against you. This chapter will show you how!

Would you like to have 15 minutes of free time every day? How about being able to get your work done early and have more spare time for leisure activities? Or what about being more productive when you are at work, and thus can *show your stuff* to get more promotions, responsibility or money? Effective time management can make the difference in your job and your life!

What are your biggest obstacles to getting the free time you need, or obstacles to keeping to your day's plan? Take a moment and write down the top ten obstacles that you typically face in your routine day that distract you from your goals. Set this list aside, and we'll come back to it later.

A minute of reflection

Time. What is it? Think about it for a minute.... Look at your wrist watch or a wall clock, wait one full minute, and see how it feels, doing nothing for a full minute!

   Tick-tock, tick-tock, tick-tock

How did that space of time feel? What are your thoughts about time, and the use of time?

One minute is a lot of time: 60 in an hour, 1,440 per day, over half a million per year. What you do with those minutes is similar to how you invest your money: it is either adding value or it is being wasted.

Time management is planning and making choices.

27

The basic concept

Let's not procrastinate any longer – let's get right to the concept of how to manage time better.

Time management is the art and science of

> **Planning**, and
>
> **Making choices**.

It's that simple.

Time management is having a plan to know what you want to accomplish, and making choices through the day, minute by minute, to check yourself against that plan in order to keep heading in the right direction. The concept is simple. Understanding the process, anticipating the potential pitfalls, and knowing how to keep on track is what we will address now to refine your tools for this task.

Planning

2,000 years ago, Seneca (4 B.C. to 65 A.D.) said

> *"Our plans miscarry because they have no aim. When a man does not know what harbor he is making for, no wind is the right wind."*

Do you know where you are headed as you start your day? How do you set your priorities? Do you have a plan for the day? Actually, the process begins with a much broader perspective. Life priorities!

Life is a balance of work, non-work (including. family, friends, hobbies, leisure, faith, etc.) and rest (sleep!). In theory, it could be 8 hours per day for each of these three basic blocks. You may distribute your time blocks (professional, personal and sleep) in different proportions, but the point is that your productivity at work or home begins first with a broader view of your life's priorities. We will review a few simple examples from home and work that will clarify how you can improve your own management of time for greater success towards achieving life goals and work goals.

A life example of planning and making choices

Let's assume that you have chosen to improve your life by following a renewed priority for health and well being. You decide to join a top-notch fitness club and want to start a diet. You commit yourself to a plan for better eating habits and exercise.

You have this vision for self-improvement. Easy, right? Why not?

Issues such as temptations, distractions, and conflicts of time all threaten your focus to stick to your plan. However, anticipating these threats to the plan allows you to develop a counter-attack.

For example, if a co-worker or friend stops by with some extra doughnuts, and offers you one, this is a time for a choice: to eat or not. The child in you likes the instant gratification. But the adult in you allows you to see the longer term vision (better health, better feeling, better looks, whatever prompted your vision and weight-loss goal to be generated in the first place), and you say to yourself, "I'll skip the doughnut so that I can keep to my master plan for health improvement."

There may be other forces at work besides the child in you, other than the need for instant gratification, which causes you to stray from the plan, or to not even try to have a plan. It is the same for many of us. Sometimes our life experiences make us feel it is futile to plan. We've had disappointments or depression so that the thought of planning seems to be more burden than benefit. In other cases, similar to sports, where not all of us are natural athletes, we just don't see ourselves as natural planners. We seem to work twice as hard as co-workers who plan and achieve things, while we struggle to develop and stick to our plan. Past experience makes us think the techniques don't really work for us, and it's not worth the effort to try.

Each of us is different. All you need to do is look at the desks at work around you, or the different rooms in your house, to see the range from order to clutter. Yet, each person has his or her own system that seems to work. That's the key point. Find what works for you and continuously improve it to make it more efficient. If you know you hate to plan, then you may have to work a bit harder than the natural planner does. However, you can do it. Making that commitment to change is the first step to effective time management. Start easy, slice the salami in some new way to set your day's priorities, and then monitor your activities that day in order to put refinements in place for tomorrow. Continue with that process and you will see the benefit. This basic approach is worth re-emphasizing:

1. Try something new (with a small slice, a small change).

2. Monitor your progress.

3. Modify as needed.

4. Repeat the cycle.

Let's continue with our hypothetical situation. You want to achieve a new level of health through a fitness plan and diet. Assume you were on your way to the fitness center. How might you react if a friend said, "Hey, do you want to go see that new movie?" Again, choices: share a good time with a friend, or keep to the master long-term plan for improved health and fitness? Success with life management is a question of having the plan, and then making choices to help stay with the plan. We see the long-term benefit as greater gratification than yielding to the temptation of the short-term distraction.

Of course, the distractions need not be only happy alternatives, such as a doughnut or a movie. Perhaps the phone rings and the distraction is that you find out that your water heater just developed a leak and it is flooding your apartment or home. Then do you still go to the gym? Of course not! Or maybe you do – but we'll get to that in a moment.

Contingency planning

You can create contingency plans in anticipation of a temptation, a happy distraction or a troublesome calamity. This plan might include being ready with a comfortable and tactful way to say "No thank you" to your friend, who wants to share his or her desserts with you, or who wants to spend time with you doing some unplanned fun activity like seeing a movie. You can also prepare contingency plans for unhappy consequences such as a leaking water heater.

For example, how old was that water heater anyway? What warning signs was it giving before it finally failed? Have you seen rusty colored water lately, or seen a few drops of water at the base of the heater? The heater becomes a crisis when it happens, out of the blue, with no warning and must be dealt with at that instant. Generally, however, you can or should have a clue about issues on the horizon or on your life's radar screen, and you can start to take preparatory action to mitigate the impact when or if these events occur.

So what about the water heater? What could have been done differently?

What if you replace the deteriorated unit when there is a sale on water heaters? This way, you do the change at lowest possible cost and at a convenient time. Also, you benefit from having the time to do any pre-purchase research, allowing you to get the best product features for lowest cost, rather than being forced to buy during a crisis. How about having a reliable plumber's phone number handy, and ask a neighbor whom you trust with the keys to your place to let the plumber in to do the job? What else might you do at the instant of the issue to let you get right back to your fitness-center plan?

The 3 Ds

Having a contingency plan, for happy or unhappy interruptions, gives you the best odds to be able to stick to your master plan. Generally, the contingency plan can fit into one of three basic options:

Delegate

Delay

Delete

Delegate: Where possible you can have someone else take care of the emergency (the plumber, the neighbor, a friend, etc.). Don't underestimate this option. Not all problems must be yours to solve. In fact, in the book "Are Your Lights On? – How to figure out what the problem *really* is.," authors Donald Gause and Gerald Weinberg explore ways to clearly define what the problem is, where does it come from, and perhaps vitally important for your own time management, whose problem is it? The monkey does *not* always need to be on your back. You can pass it to the proper owner to stay on track with your own plans and effective use of your time.

Delay: Respond to the immediate issue, but delay the time consuming details for later. You can shut off the water supply to stop the flow, throw down some towels to absorb what's there now, and then do the tank replacement later, after you have completed your original plan.

Delete: Ignore it (move to another apartment!). This option will not work for all cases, but we will soon see how it can be used more often than you think.

An easy way to remember this time-management concept is simply to recognize that you can pass a problem on to someone better suited to deal with it, you can do it later, or you don't have to do it at all. These simple options, the three Ds, are powerful ways to manage your time more productively.

A fourth D could be *distraction*, which is often what ends up being the knee-jerk reaction (you stop what you are doing, interrupt your plan, and take care of the emergency of the moment). This "D" is not a contingency plan, but instead is what keeps us from staying on track. Our time management techniques will allow us to avoid this "D." Try to find one of the first three Ds as your primary route to success rather than needlessly default to the fourth D.

The same process is in place in a work environment. Distractions are doughnuts! We need to learn to recognize the hidden time-wasters, which work against our plan for the day. So let's probe this issue in greater detail, starting with the planning process at work, before we talk more about your choices.

Planning at work

Of course, the plans start with your vision for the longer term – maybe retirement and working back from there. But shorter term your planning process should include goals for the next few years, then shorter range, to one year, one month, one week, and finally for today. All of this should fit together with your personal priorities and those of the company.

Your work goals should be *SMART goals*: **S**pecific (clear definition of the task and result), **M**easurable (quantifiable targets rather than *motherhood and apple pie* generalities), **A**chievable (realistic), **R**elevant (add value to you and the organization), and **T**imed (have a deadline or expected steps with timing for completion). It's best if they are written and your supervisor is in agreement with these tasks and targets. You can find a lot more detail on the Internet about SMART and DUMB goals (discussed later) if you need more clarity on this topic of setting properly structured goals. The point is that you base your plan on specific tasks geared to meet goals and objectives that you have set.

Have you considered meeting with your boss to discuss these goals? Make sure you have alignment with the company objectives, and in particular your supervisor's expectations of what is needed. These goals can include elements of personal growth for your own development and simultaneously contribute to the company's success. It's okay to have work goals that directly benefit you, aside from accruing benefits to your company. Perhaps it is a goal that lets you get experience with constructing an annual budget, or managing a major project for the first time. Establish your plan by thinking about what you need to achieve for your longer-term personal objectives as well as what is needed for improvements in your department for the coming year.

Starting from annual goals that are consistent with the company plans, your supervisor's expectations, and your own desires for departmental and personal improvement, you can focus on shorter-term actions for quarterly and monthly targets. Ultimately, this goal and planning process works itself naturally to a daily plan.

The best time and way to prepare your daily plan

When is the best time to lay out your daily plan? Is it the night before or in the morning, before you start your work? What approach should you use to have the daily plan in front of you, such as checklists, calendar notes or computer generated reminders?

The answer: It really doesn't matter. What does matter is that you **have** a plan, and that you **stick to the routine religiously!** The night before, or in the morning, using to-do lists or stacks of papers, all can work, if you know it works for you, and you **follow this plan every day without fail.**

What systems work for you? Options can include use of hand-held personal electronic reminder devices, lists of things to do, file systems for 31 days of the month and 12 months of the year, organization of the desk or desk calendar, keeping paper handy for making notes of things that need to be done, a daily system of checking and re-checking where you stand on your day's priorities, use of the computer for instant reminders that tell you it's time to do something, and asking someone to help you with your plans.

How can you find or develop a system that will work for you? Try several, and pick the best elements that seem to fit with your personality and your approach to daily activities. Talk to friends at work who seem to have it all together, or neighbors whose life-style and organization skills you admire. Ask them about their systems. Find out what they've tried before, and why they settled on their particular planning and tracking system. Those who are already successful in planning and follow-up techniques can provide useful insights for you to evaluate and to try. Tailor the system so it works for you. Modify the system until you find it functions in your real world. Then stick to it!

Do you have a follow-up system that works well enough to assure that you would remember to do a task in the future, such as three years from now, on this same date, at 2 o'clock in the afternoon? Why is follow-up important and why should you have a system that works to remind you of tasks when you need to be reminded? We'll discuss follow-up processes and priority in more detail in Chapter 12 ("Don't Forget!"), but for now let's at least understand its importance and relevance to time management.

Track your results

An important component of time management, and ultimately successful productivity on the job or at home, is to have systems that consistently work for you to track follow-up items. These techniques are important for company, peer, boss and client respect and confidence, as well as for friends or family members who count on you to do what you say you will do. Also, your use of reliable follow-up systems allows you to have fun with birthday and anniversary reminders, and those extra personal touches that become memorable. In addition, your follow-up can assure that you stick to practical housekeeping tasks such as backing up your computer files, doing disk clean up and defragging your hard drive on a regular basis. Managing follow-up is a part of managing time.

More strategies

Strategies for task management should include trying to do the important or most difficult tasks first, so that you have the most time to keep going back to them if you do get interrupted. Also, as you accomplish each task, the next task on the list is easier, and finally the last items on your list become rewards, almost the same as dessert after a meal. If you've first eaten your vegetables, you can then have your cake and ice cream afterwards!

Get the tough jobs done first, and enjoy the others next. At the end of each day, you will have completed all the critical tasks and perhaps a few fun ones too. Your approach should also include routinely and frequently re-assessing your status during the day, to allow you to evaluate your progress with your list of things that need doing.

So, we have our plan for the day. We're set, right? Wrong! Now it's time to anticipate and respond appropriately to the doughnuts! In come the distractions and emergencies. How can we deal with those?

Choices

Distractions come in all forms. It's a telephone call when you are deep into a conversation or a project. It's a person who stops to ask for your help while you are knee-deep in a hot assignment. It may be a neighbor who unexpectedly drops over to chat when you are trying to get things ready before dinner. It's a client who needs your services just at the moment you were set to tackle a touchy task. Or it's a call from nature.

We don't live and work in a vacuum, and at work we are paid to be problem solvers who provide service to our organization and clients. Thus, our role is not to be self-focused, working only on our personal daily tasks, but rather to serve the needs of the organization and client. However, our to-do list for the day hopefully is geared to meeting these organization, client and personal objectives anyway. Accordingly, the issue of distraction is one of putting the interruption to the plan in perspective with the long-term and short-term objectives.

In time management, we must evaluate whether satisfying the immediate crisis or interruption is in line with, or in opposition to, the missions, visions or goals that we hope to achieve this day.

Interruptions and distractions at home or work

At the beginning of this chapter, I asked you to create a list of your top ten obstacles to effective time management, at home or at work, which you face in a routine day. Let's look at that list now.

How might you employ strategies of the three Ds (Delegation, Delay, Delete)? How might you use the strategy of contingency planning (anticipate the interruption, and have a plan ready to put in place, so that this distraction will have a reduced impact on your initial plan for the day) in order to return to your plan as quickly as possible?

Let's consider the option of *delete* with additional clarity. Maybe you need to delete a task, or "delete" an interruption.

Sometimes the task we have listed to do, and keep deferring, should simply be deleted from our list. It may not be that important after all. Similarly, an interruption by someone with his or her hot and urgent problem can sometimes be dismissed (deleted) as well. Maybe all you need to do is have a short explanation that honestly says to the person who has interrupted your plan: "I appreciate your concern, but this is just something that we, the company, are not able to address, and can not do. Perhaps we will be able to deal with this at another time, but it is not now consistent with our values, priorities, or plans. Sorry but we can not take on your request." Not all interruptions must be resolved. But, they all have to be dealt with somehow (including deletion, as one of the three Ds).

Before going on, I just want to touch on this "delete" option a bit deeper, since it seems so contrary to our natural leadership "can-do" instincts. We will discuss further in the next chapter about the importance of a can-do attitude. This personality characteristic also appears in chapters 15 and 16, where you learn about communicating your skills during the job interview. Nonetheless, a good leader has to use all the tools available, when appropriate, to be as effective as possible. One of these tools is to know when and how to say "No." When it comes to time management, be sure to use this "delete" tool when necessary.

Urgent versus Important

This is a key distinction. Important tasks often get bumped aside, superseded by an urgent need. However, if the urgent item is not also important, the choice to deal with it may be ill-founded. Issues are often important to other people, but not to your overall plan or the company's needs. Simply because the issue arrives at your door or desk with a sense of urgency, does not automatically mean that it is important enough to destroy your master plan for the day or the important task you are currently working to resolve.

Caution: as you work the strategies for keeping to your plan, you must be sure that you are satisfying the overall objectives of your company, your supervisor, your family and your reason for being in your current role. You do not want to have your peers, supervisor, clients, family, friends or others feel rejected as you selfishly stick to your plan for the day.

George Bernard Shaw, the famous Irish playwright, said:

"To the person with a toothache, even if the world is tottering, there is nothing more important than a visit to a dentist."

If you are that dentist (that is, the problem solver), the person with the problem does not want to feel that you have turned him or her away simply to enable you to meet your daily targets for personal productivity! You don't want to leave the impression with the person who comes to you for help, that you are one of those individuals who wear a hat with the statement, "You must have me confused with someone who gives a damn!"

Regardless of your pressing priorities or personal time-management plan, you still should take a moment to at least acknowledge the other person's need for help. Either re-direct this person to someone who can help (Delegate; I can not or will not do it, but someone else can do it for you), or give an honest statement of what you plan to do. This may be to say, "I will address this later," (Delay) or "I will not be able to give this a priority at all due to other pressing matters," (Delete) with as tactful and a courteous letdown as you possibly can.

There is a balance that must be struck between sticking to your time-management plan versus diverting from your plan to handle real crisis management issues, or to work on matters that are both urgent and important. You must be able to distinguish between what really has to be addressed, and other less critical situations. Manage both the *distractions* and the *urgent-but-not-important* issues with the three Ds.

The balance between our focus on goals, both company and personal, and how we deal with the unexpected events that pop up, can be a real test of our time management skills. Thinking about the routines that flow through our normal day, those routines that are imposed on us as well as the routines that we impose on ourselves, can help improve our use of time. This also includes private time, for planning, dreaming and doing. Having a plan and making choices to stick to the plan are keys to time management. Let's dig a bit further now into the process we can follow to have better success with our use of time.

Visualize an hourglass, dropping sand, Ferris wheel and gears

We are all familiar with the conversion of power that comes from a typical river and water wheel system, taking the energy from a slow moving stream and allowing the water to drop into buckets aligned along the circumference of a wheel. In turn, the rotation of the wheel drives gears that allow work to be done, such as grinding grain into flour. I'd like you now to visualize that the *energy* or *power* contained in the upper half of an hourglass is just another way to represent the power of time. It either works for you or against you.

Think of the impact and use of time as though you were using the sand that flows through the top half of a giant hourglass. Position this imaginary source of sand (time) so that when the sand exits from the bottle-neck of the hour glass it falls directly into buckets where the passenger seats normally are, on the circumference of a Ferris wheel. The wheel in turn is connected to a series of gears and belts.

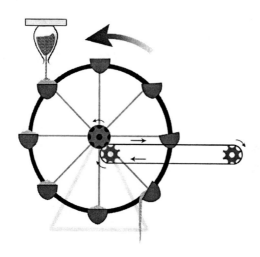

Let the "power of time" work for you.

What happens? As the sand drops from the hourglass, the buckets fill. With their added weight, they move down, causing the Ferris wheel to rotate. This creates action in the gears connected to the wheel and produces some desired mechanical result. The gears and belts transmit this motion into other useful energy. You use the sand to move the gears and belt. In this analogy, time has been productively converted into work.

For the purpose of this mental image (and graphic) I have elected to empty each bucket near the bottom so that each bucket gets ready for a refill the next time it reaches the top. Don't be distracted with worrying about the mechanics of how all this structural stuff works. I'm only trying to help you visualize your role to manage your use of time and to use it constructively. This bucket emptying can also reinforce the message that "Time runs out!" Make sure you make the best use of time when you have it. You only go around once.

Your placement and pre-arrangement of the hourglass, buckets and gears is the equivalent of your time-management plan: a way to make your use of time, the movement of the sand, turn into desired results. You decide in advance what needs to be done, and in what order.

I've heard it said that

> *"Managers are good at getting things done, but Leaders are good at knowing what needs to be done."*

The implication is that any manager can follow orders, and get things done, but leadership involves the capability of having vision for what is important, and setting a plan in place to get it done. In your role as a leader, you need to have vision, set priorities and develop a plan to accomplish your goals. Then you need to be able to stick to the plan to get the intended results.

Baffling

With this hourglass and Ferris wheel analogy, the distractions you face are equivalent to baffles placed between the dropping sand and the rotating buckets. What happens as each of the buckets awaits a new charge of sand to keep the wheel of progress rotating? These baffles divert the sand from flowing into your pre-arranged buckets. As a result, the buckets, the wheel and gears sit idle, waiting for the falling sand.

Unfortunately, the sand never enters the buckets. The sand has instead been deflected, thereby stopping the wheel's movement, just as distractions deflect you from your plan. The belts and gears don't turn, and your mechanism comes to a grinding halt: No action, no work, no productivity. The potential energy from the falling sand is diverted to other tasks, instead of helping the wheel to move.

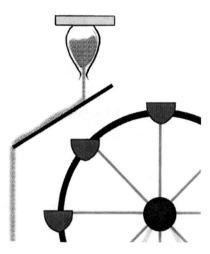

Don't be baffled! Learn to control distractions.

Will you see the baffles when they come? Will you know how to react to minimize their influence on your plan? Our earlier discussion covered the important topics of setting SMART long-term goals, bringing that down to daily lists of prioritized things to be accomplished, and using techniques (the 3-Ds and contingency plans) to minimize the negative impact from distractions. However, you have to realize that distractions can occur at any moment, and your plan must include how to deal with the distractions to remain focused on the day's original objectives.

Staying on track

The process of having your vision, setting a plan, and prioritizing includes the following eight essential steps:

- Analyze – set the priority for what needs to be done (tasks, problems to solve, steps in your goal, timing).

- Organize – get the work plan set.

- Leverage – think about who can best get the job done (it doesn't always need you; delegate).

- Monitor – continuously watch your progress through the day versus the plan.

- Re-evaluate – consider your priorities and overall plans based on timing and results to the moment.

- Re-group – change the plans for the balance of the day based on your status.

- Focus – do what is necessary to get the job done with minimum distractions.

- Balance – take a break, breathe deeply, smell the roses, laugh, smile, enjoy (you may discover a better fresh idea or unique solution to your problems once you step away for a moment).

Then, step back and begin the cycle again.

In the midst of this process of planning and following through on the plan with proper choices, be ever vigilant to recognize baffles or distractions when they occur, and make the right choices to stay on track.

What else can we do to improve our odds of effective time management?

Routines

Every day has its routines. Some are imposed on us, and some routines we impose on ourselves. How we manage our routines also contributes to effective time management. What are some routines imposed on your day? These can include activities such as staff meetings and obligations for repetitive reports. How can you manage your time better with these impositions?

Have you considered options such as these?

1. Reduce the time or frequency of the routine meetings.

2. Request that participants in regular meetings become responsible for improved pre-meeting preparations that will save time during the meeting.

3. Improve productivity in a meeting by providing reading materials to participants before the meeting, which covers discussion topics.

4. Require participants to submit input about a topic to the meeting coordinator ahead of time, rather than waiting for the meeting itself to blab on about the issue.

5. Have structure to the meetings with time limits and agendas published ahead of time.

6. Offer suggestions to the meeting's host to modify the time, frequency, topics, and preparation to make better use of time for all attendees, even if you do not run the meetings.

Regarding routine reports, formats can be standardized, data can be gathered by others, or at best, some reports may be eliminated. Does each document still add value? If not, get rid of it.

A basic rule: You should question the need for all meetings and reports. If needed, question the length and frequency. Then look for ways to streamline all of these to meet the objective in a more efficient way. And do this again about every 6 or 12 months. Continuous improvement in methods and productivity is a key leadership trait. The minutes you save add up, as you invest your time more wisely.

What about routines which are self-imposed? What meetings do you set? What about lunch, coffee breaks, reports that you initiate, etc.? What can you change, once you start to look at this use of time carefully? At home, what TV programs do you enjoy, and how many hours do they consume? Is there a better way to watch them (such as the use of TiVo to skip all the commercials, instead of watching them live)?

What may not easily be recognized about self-imposed routines is how you react to certain actions in your daily routine.

Ring!

When the phone rings what do you do? Do you answer the phone? Do you have to? What might you be doing when the phone is ringing? How will this impact your plan or accomplishments?

When nature calls, we often *hold it* until we have a convenient time to take a break. Yet when a phone rings, we often stop everything, put the world on hold, and answer the phone. Why is that?

We impose this interruption on our work process by ourselves. We create our own interruption.

Know thyself. Deep down, many of us thrive on being problem solvers; being the one everybody comes to for the answer, or holding all the cards to be in the key position for action. Our rewards come from fighting the fire, solving the crisis, or being the center of action. This can be fun.

This behavior also can be a great detraction from getting important plans done during the day, since some of us are instant-gratification and action-oriented, rather than planned and controlled managers of our time. It may not be as much fun organizing a good plan and then calmly carrying it out, but it sure is effective, and ultimately does more good for the organization and ourselves. It may not be as much fun passing up the doughnut, but it is the right thing to do to meet your long-term fitness and health plan.

Speaking about effectiveness, it probably warrants a brief comment about the difference between efficiency and effectiveness. Sometimes people focus upon having an efficient plan, or routines that they are proud of, with well-honed steps that reduce waste. They enjoy the efficiency with which they get the job done. However, the outcome of the task itself may not contribute much to achieving overall goals, and thus is not effective in producing results.

Our work must be effective, not just efficient. Reducing waste and improving productivity is fine, but that work itself must move the organization forward to the intended goals. A fuel-efficient car may use fewer miles per gallon, but may be ineffective in pulling heavy loads, which needs a strong and sturdy pick-up truck. Time management includes knowing what to do, how to do it efficiently, with as little waste as possible, and knowing how to do it effectively, thereby getting to the intended result as quickly as possible.

You can leverage your time management with proper use of imposed and self-imposed routines. Not all self-imposed routines are bad. Here is an important one to cultivate:

Private time

Start small and gradually grow the self-imposed use of private time to plan. Perhaps begin with once per week, on a Friday afternoon, when things at work may be winding down (or whenever may be the slower time in your work environment or culture). Take 15 minutes just for yourself: no phone calls, no meetings, no interruptions allowed! If necessary, close your door, transfer your phone or shut it off.

Use this time to review your long-term and short-term goals. Set up your plan for the next week. Reflect on your accomplishments of the past week and where you need to go to keep things on track. Don't get all caught up on any failings, but rather focus on what went right and what you need to do to tune-up your next 5 to 7 work days. For whatever did go wrong, think ahead about how you might handle a similar situation in the future to get better results. Use your system to list your tasks and priorities coming up, so you are set to hit the next week running!

Full circle:

This brings us full circle. You need a **plan** for the day that is **linked** to your life plans and to your organization's plans. The daily plan should be **prioritized**, so you can strive to assure the most important things get done first, or by the end of the day, by making **choices** of what to do when. You may or may not have completed the things you wanted to do, but at least you have completed the tasks that **had** to be done. You should **anticipate and recognize interruptions** when they occur, and **have a plan ready** for how to deal with the most common interruptions, using the strategy of the three Ds (Delegate, Delay, Delete), contingency plans or other alternatives.

Whatever system you use for daily planning and time management, you should **use your system faithfully and consistently**, including follow-up. Finally, you should **be sensitive to the manner in which you exercise your time management actions** to support the goals of your company or household, your supervisor's or family's expectations and your own objectives **without damaging the feelings of your customers, boss, peers or clients, family or friends**.

Re-**check your status several times a day**, and at the end of the day (or the next morning) get yourself set for the next day's plan. **At least once per week set your private time for reflection and planning**. Eventually, you will be able to fit in more daily private time (instead of weekly), and a bit longer monthly and quarterly planning sessions for yourself.

Before you know it, there won't be as many crises to solve. You may get those 15 free minutes, or more, every day, and then the promotion at work and the best vacation for you and the family! The tick-tock, tick-tock, tick-tock of the clock is now your opportunity for success as you make the most of every minute.

Perhaps you are now saying to yourself, "I'll never have the time to be able to make these changes to my routine," or you are saying, "This is great! With these techniques I can finally change my control of time and my future!" It's all a question of attitude, the theme of Chapter 4.

Chapter 4

They Don't Wear Shoes

Have you heard the story about the two sales representatives?

There's a tale about the sales manager of a shoe company who wanted to expand internationally. He called his two newest sales representatives to his office to explain his market research interest and the role that each of them will play for setting a new sales strategy for the company.

He explained the following plan to them: "Our company has been focused domestically for the last several years, but it's time to see if we have any opportunities to sell our shoes in new parts of the world. I want each of you to go to Zinzapato for two weeks, explore the opportunities in this undeveloped country and call me back to let me know your recommendations."

Inspired with the challenge and the responsibility that was given to them, the two sales representatives eagerly set out for Zinzapato. They spent their two weeks independently viewing the people, their habits, and assessing the likelihood of selling their company's shoes to this potential market.

When the two weeks were up, they each made their call back to the home office with their recommendation.

The first sales representative called the boss and said, "Sorry, Boss. After two weeks of study it's clear to me we have no chance whatsoever to sell our shoes here. In fact, I'll tell you how bad it is: they don't even wear shoes here!"

Moments later the second sales representative made her call to the boss and enthusiastically exclaimed, "What a great opportunity, Boss! We should start our sales plan here immediately. It's fantastic! Let me tell you how good it is: they don't even wear shoes here!"

What's the lesson from this imaginary tale? It all depends on your point of view. Attitude makes the difference. Both sales representatives saw the same evidence, people without shoes, but each interpreted the data through his or her own personal filter for analysis, which in turn biased their conclusions. One saw the lack of wearing shoes as a sure sign that the people had no interest in foot coverings, yet the other saw this situation as unlimited potential to cover all those bare feet with their company's product. How you view the situation is the first step in the process to make things happen. Some people view the obstacles, when others view the opportunity. It's a question of attitude, a key characteristic for success.

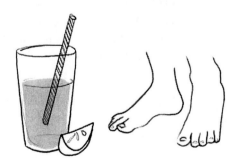

What's your attitude?

Half empty or half full?

It's the basic question of whether the glass is half empty or half full. Do you look at things on the bright side, optimistically, or do you see all the negatives of a situation and pessimistically shape your action plan accordingly? Your view of the reality shapes your actions. It's often a natural reaction, probably based on how we were brought up as children combined with the years of conditioning that have molded our interpretation of events in our life to be hopeful or skeptical, eager or fearful, trusting or cynical.

Consider these two contradictory views of life situations or surroundings:

> *"A cynic is a man who, when he smells flowers, looks around for the coffin."* (H. L. Mencken)

> *"Things turn out best for those who make the best of the way things turn out."* (Art Linkletter)

What's your first natural reaction to situations? A good manager works to realistically evaluate the data, trying to be as objective as possible, weighing the risks and benefits in order to insure that important decisions are not just based on emotion or hopes, but instead upon facts, data and reason. Good leaders, however, must remain sensitive to their own styles and, as necessary, double-check natural reactions that influence their perception of reality. If you know you tend to see the bright side, perhaps you need to take a moment to assure you are properly analyzing the potential risks of a project. Conversely, if you tend to look at the dark side of most issues, try to open yourself up to the possibilities of upside potential.

My experience, however, has shown that those with the positive *can do* attitude, willing to take on risks because they *know* they can make it work, and they see the opportunities where others only see the risk, more often are the winners. You can develop this positive self-confidence and can-do attitude through attention to your daily habits and perspectives. The record breakers and pioneers in their fields, pushing the envelope of knowledge and results, do not give up in the face of what others feel are impossible odds, because the inner voice of these achievers tells them that they will succeed.

Having said that, one contrary position that I too support is expressed in the book "Mark H. McCormack – On Managing" (published by Random House Business Books. Reprinted by permission of The Random House Group Ltd.). The author dedicates one section with this heading: "Pessimism Pays When It Comes To Time." McCormack states :

> "The awful truth is, we tend to be optimistic rather than pessimistic about how much we can accom-plish in a day – and it costs us. Our inflated opti-mism irritates people, disappoints others, and in extreme cases ruins our credibility.

> "The quick cure, obviously, is to err on the side of pessimism in gauging our use of time."

The author continues with an example where you have a meeting across town, and you think that you can get there in 20 minutes (with an optimistic view, making all the traffic lights and no tie-ups en route). He suggests that instead you allow a half hour *just in case*. Taking this pessimistic view of time will allow you to meet your obligations more consistently. Speaking about commitments, and attitude, please consider the following.

"Try to do it" versus "Do it"

How do you respond to a task to do something? Do you say "I'll try to do it for you," or do you say, "I will do it"? There's a big difference. *Trying* implies effort but no commitment. If it all goes sour, the response can be, "Well, I did try, but sorry - no results." We are measured on our results, not our efforts! I had a supervisor who wrote the following formula on the board for all of us to see:

$$Results \neq No\ Results + Excuses$$

The word "Results" does *not* equal "No results plus excuses." His point was, "I want results, not excuses." Saying you *tried* is not the same as saying *you did it.* Consider any of the following statements from this perspective and see how little is being committed when someone says:

I will try to….

- Call you tomorrow at 10:00 a.m.

- Get the report to you in two weeks.

- Pick up the groceries on the way home.

- Clean up the living room before our company comes for dinner.

Leaders are measured on results, not wishes, intentions or promises. Similarly, they are remembered for their delivery on commitments. Eliminate the phrase "I will try" from your vocabulary. Replace it with "I will…." Begin with the mind-set that you will, and you will. Begin with the attitude that you will try, and there's a good chance that you've already given yourself the excuse that you don't have to actually do it, since all you promised was that you would try. Make it a personal code of honor that your word has value, and that you meet your obligations.

A question of control

You may be saying to yourself, "How can I commit to the result when I don't have full control of the circumstances?" You're right. Sometimes there are variables that prevent our 100% control. Frankly, that is more often the rule than the exception. However, you have at least two ways to manage the situation.

One way to increase your ability to make commitments happen is to provide a reasonable time frame, up-front, giving yourself sufficient slack-time to make adjustments in the face of unforeseen events. This was discussed above when McCormack suggested taking the pessimistic view of time, to give yourself added time for the things that might go wrong.

The other alternative is to act promptly, when you see some potential delay in your delivery of the promise. Simply get back to the person to whom you made your commitment. You can give an update of expectations when you tell them about your new potential completion time, but do this early enough to allow this person to provide you with new input on priorities or perhaps added resources to get the task done when originally committed

Don't tell the person at the last moment, "Sorry, my task will not be ready for you this afternoon as originally promised a month ago." Instead, when you first see that the original commitment may be unreachable, days in advance, you should alert your customer (boss, peer, spouse, friend or client) to the potential problem. In effect, you renegotiate a new commitment date: either you can meet your new schedule, or you can adjust priorities and resources with the other person's input that will still allow project completion when originally forecasted.

In the end, when you say you will do something, you do it. Your record of accomplishment builds confidence in others. Your reputation for results builds itself. Others have a positive attitude about you, and you have a positive attitude about yourself.

Your attitude impacts the results of others

It's all about you. Aside from your own self-confidence that is enhanced as you focus on your positive results when you adhere to meeting commitments and as you appreciate your own good progress, those around you also respond to and reflect your attitude.

When the boss comes storming into the office, grumbling about the terrible traffic, the bad weather, or the poor results of the company, everyone ducks for cover! No one wants to end up in his or her sights, a target for wrath today. However, bright people, who share their smiles and positive reinforcement, bring out the best in others. Your attitude impacts others. Make a conscious choice to be more positive, and less reminiscent of the supervisor who makes the team shudder. Your actions can be uplifting or can sink the team spirit. Tune in to how your attitude is helpful or hurtful to others.

For this reason, it is critical what type of person is at the top of an organization. A friend of mine knows the importance of this characteristic, and factors such behavior into his job selection process.

A true story

A great "attitude" comment I heard recently surfaced during a conversation with my friend Fred Hagan. He and I worked together in 1990, and during a vacation visit to us he told me about his experience interviewing a candidate for the position of general manager of a Hampton Inn hotel that Fred and seven other partners own in Martin, Tennessee.

A candidate, Dana Davis, had been working for another Hampton Inn for 11 years, and at the time of the interview was their front desk manager. Fred wanted to learn more about her experience dealing with those unexpected problems that pop-up in the middle of the night, and whenever Murphy's Laws are working against you.

As Fred and Dana talked about these typical difficulties, and how to deal with the problems, Dana remarked, "The words *"I can't"* won't come out of my mouth!" Now how's that for attitude? You can just visualize this *can-do* person tackling whatever comes at her, with spirit, with an eager customer focus and, like a dog with a bone, unable to let go until the problem has been solved satisfactorily. She just would not say, "I can't," without trying something else to resolve a problem and satisfy a customer. Dana would see what she *can do* to win the hearts of her customers.

Now that's the kind of person I'd want on my team. Apparently, it's also the kind of person that Fred and the other owners of the Inn wanted on theirs. Dana got the job!

Another positive attitude person

During my university days, I had the pleasure to know Terry Orlick. He was captain of our university gymnastics team one year ahead of me, so we were close through our daily workouts, lots of talking time, and even a memorable spring-break marathon car trip from Syracuse, New York, to Sarasota, Florida, for a weeklong gymnastics camp. He was always an *up* person, who focused on the simple joys of life and made you feel good about yourself when in his presence. He went on to earn a Ph.D., specializing in behavioral excellence. As a professor in this field at the University of Ottawa in Canada, Terry has written many books on the topic. Excerpts from the back of one of his books, "Embracing Your Potential," describe Terry this way:

> "When the first-ever all-women's team was selected for the America's Cup, the athletes were told they could select anyone in the world to work with them on strengthening their mental game. They chose Terry Orlick.

> "Around the world, athletes, coaches, teachers, and performers know Terry Orlick as "the best" in his field. .... He has worked with thousands of Olympic and professional athletes, great surgeons, astronauts, top classical musicians, opera singers, dancers, performing artists, trial lawyers, business

executives, mission control personnel, and others engaged in high stress careers.

"Terry is President of the International Society for Mental Training and Excellence and has received the highest award for excellence in teaching. He is author of more than twenty highly acclaimed books and has created innovative programs for children and youth to develop humanistic perspectives and positive mental skills for living."

Terry's natural positive attitude was contagious when we were at Syracuse University together, and still is. A leader with his characteristics makes you want to do more. Such a leader's positive reinforcement keeps moving you to higher levels of performance. This leader's attitude makes a difference in your life.

I particularly enjoyed reading some of Terry's comments in his book, "Embracing Your Potential," related to attitude, and I close this chapter with his perspectives:

"Life is what you dwell on. If you dwell on the negative, life is negative. If you dwell on the positive, life is positive."

"So much of staying positive is acquiring a perspective that allows us to find something positive in the situations we face. A positive attitude lifts all people, in the same way that a rising tide lifts all boats."

Your attitude can change not only your life, but can change the lives of many others as well. We will further address this issue of change in our next chapter.

How can you be a change maker? That's the focus of Chapter 5.

Chapter 5

Be a Change Maker

Three key questions

Most of what is covered in this book is based on topics I've developed and presented in seminars, workshops and lectures in the United States, Chile and Brazil. I did these for businesses, ranging from large international corporations to smaller family-owned operations, and in the academic world for courses I've taught in university settings, schools for English as a Second Language, and other career preparatory venues. Despite the differences in cultures and context, or language and location, the responses I get to three key questions associated with the theme of this chapter are surprisingly similar. The importance of the issues and the enlightenment that follows comes to the core of the change process.

Question one: Does anybody have change for a dollar?

To warm-up my audience, I pull a dollar bill from my pocket (or in the case of Chile, it's a *luca,* the slang for the 1,000 peso Chilean note, or the *real,* Brazil's currency). Raising the bill high over my head, I ask the question, "Does anybody have change for a dollar?" I then explain that it's a contest. The first person to bring his or her change to me gets a small prize. It's fun from the podium to see the audience participants scrambling in their purses and pockets to win the undefined award.

In a moment, a winner usually rushes forward and I give this eager person my promised trinket of relatively insignificant financial value (perhaps a ballpoint pen, or souvenir from an out-of-country location). The winner beams, we all have a good laugh, and then I ask, "What is the message from this exercise?"

After giving them a chance to think about this, I respond: "Those who make change are the winners of various kinds of rewards, and particularly those who can do it quickly, ahead of the competition. Today the reward was but a trinket; however in a real world environment, the change makers may reap great rewards for their company and for themselves." In the business world, the reward can be project success, financial growth, recognition and promotions. On the personal side, the rewards can be self-satisfaction of a task well done, family security, and tranquility with loving and lasting relationships.

Are you a change maker?

Of course, we are now talking about "making change" as influencing or modifying the state of some condition, rather than providing coins in exchange for a dollar bill. Change of attitude, change of practices or procedures, change of habits, change of focus, or any change that can bring about business or personal improvement involves a change process.

Techniques to improve the efficiency and effectiveness of this process may vary. It is my intent to share practical techniques that allow you to make change more rapidly, with fewer disturbances and more acceptances, and to make changes that will be longer lasting. The change makers, leaders of new directions, whether at work or at home, are the ones this book is intended to help.

On the job, at home, and in most of what we do in our lives, change is constant. Advances in technology, techniques and teaching allow us (and our competitors) to find quicker, cheaper and better ways to make our products. If we are content with our position and status quo, others are likely to pass us by.

It's as though we are all traveling in the current of a river. Some swim in the direction of the flow and move faster than the river itself while some relax and paddle in place, at pace with the gradual forward movement of the general mass.

In the business world, we all benefit simultaneously from system improvements; we advance with the stream, as technology moves us all forward: telephones, fax machines, copy machines, computers, digital cameras, internet, email, net meetings (inter-office meetings held by way of the Internet, with voice, video and PowerPoint presentations shared on computer screens), hand-held devices, or whatever is the next invention to touch our lives. This push of energy moves us all forward.

Of course, some fight the current. They still love their typewriter; they'll never carry a cell phone. They may survive, but the odds are against them if their business depends on speed, service and the support of up-to-date information.

Some take note of their movement in the river of change around them. They watch the stationary landscape on the riverbank or they focus on their relative position in the midst of others moving along with them, continually measuring their forward advance. They are able to assess their relative progress.

How's your movement along the river of progress?

In addition, those who keep an eye on the competition floating along with them, are in a better position to decide the right course of action to take. If your objective is to get downstream ahead of your competition, then you'd better begin paddling now! Occasionally, successful contrarians go against the flow, or take a completely new direction, such as inventors or those with unusual personality traits. Know where you are, and where you want to go.

You can change your stroke, such as trying new techniques to reach your objective more quickly, and you can let technology be your engine of change, such as by putting on flippers to get more thrust. You can choose or modify your approach to strategic advancement. But the common denominator is that those who find the ways to effectively implement change in their organization or their lives are more likely to see the reward of this effort. Change makers win.

Question two: How many of you are in charge of one or more persons?

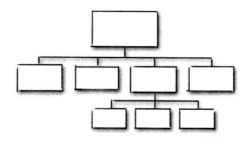

A typical organization chart

Here I ask for a show of hands of those in charge of one or more persons, and normally about half the group raises their hands, thereby distinguishing themselves as members of one of two categories. One group identifies themselves with those whose jobs are in line management, with either small or large numbers of individuals under their responsibility. They all have their hands up in the air. The other group identifies themselves as individual contributors, having functional responsibility for important tasks, such as accounting, engineering, computer technology, sales, human resources, or any one of a number of vital services, but they do not supervise anyone, so they keep their hands down.

I then take a few moments here to ask about the differences between line and staff jobs, between direct chain of command versus functional influence. Perhaps I might have fun with this example: In a family situation, the man of the family may think he is in charge, is the one who makes all the big decisions and has the final say. I know how it works in my case. I explain that my wife, Margy, is used to me having the last word: "Yes, dear." I may have the final say, but it's simply to agree with her request! Whoever is the decision maker, or however the process works at home or in the business environment, the process of change requires leadership. Anyone can become a leader of change. A leader is the person responsible for initiating change and for getting the rest to follow.

Other parts of this book address more specific and particular concepts or techniques for change, such as the "Slice the Salami" approach (Chapter 1), and the importance of establishing a sense of urgency with "See the Flames and Smell the Smoke" (Chapter 2). In addition, we will address teamwork (Chapter 8), communication skills (part of Chapter 2), the four-to-one rule (Chapter 9), and the process of "Three Eyes" (Chapter 14). But before all that detail, the point here is to understand that to make change happen, someone normally has to modify behaviors. Our first thought is often, "How can I change the behavior of others so that they will do what's needed to make change happen?" Or people think to themselves "If only I were in charge, I could just demand the change and, as the boss, the others would have to obey." Keep dreaming!

A trick question

This brings us back to the show of hands. I explain to the group that all of them should have raised their hands. Why? Because, it's a trick question. Every one of them is in charge of at least one person: themselves.

You are your own boss. You can make, and have to make, decisions that influence your own behaviors. You can change yourself. Change can be a slow process, one slice at a time, or depending on circumstances, you may have to make your changes more dramatically. In turn, the changes you make can affect others around you. Your skill improvements in topics such as time management, communications and motivational leadership are tools for more effective results. It is comparable to shifting the leverage point so that the movement you make on your side of the fulcrum creates a greater range of motion on the other side. As you hone your skills, you are creating more leverage and influence in your surroundings. Your efforts create more results as you become more proficient.

Think about the seesaw. If the fulcrum is in the middle, the other end of the seesaw moves through a path that is the same as the range of motion on your side. You move your side up and down a foot, and the other side moves up and down the same distance. If, however, the pivot point were closer to you, the movement on your end, for example one foot up and down, creates greater amplification of the range of movement on the other end of the seesaw, perhaps three or four feet, depending on just where you have placed the fulcrum.

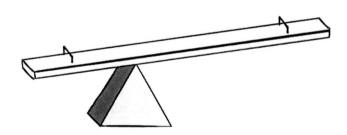

Leadership leverage amplifies results.

Learning techniques for change and learning how to change your own behaviors are akin to learning how to shift the pivot point: you get greater movement on the other side for smaller movement on your side. Over time, as if you were gradually shifting that pivot point closer to you, the same movement by you gradually creates more and more movement on the other end.

The physicists out there will no doubt be thinking now about the forces that must be the same regardless of where the pivot point is if the system is to remain in balance. In other words, when the pivot is in the middle, there is equal force on both sides to keep the seesaw stable. But if you move that fulcrum closer to you, although the other side will swing a wider arc, it takes more effort, force or pressure on your side, to balance the weight at the longer distance from the pivot on the other side of the seesaw. You have to push harder to offset the leverage of the other side.

I am convinced that the techniques you learn, the concepts from these chapters, are an investment that serves as your added force. You've built up your leadership technique muscles so that the force you apply to the seesaw feels as easy as it did before, even though you are putting more pressure to bear on your side of the fulcrum. Let's call that "leadership leverage." What you see are the fruits of your labor with the added movement and increased reaction on the other side of the seesaw. You will make change happen with more ease as time and technique move forward. You initiate actions with what feels as though they are simply small nudges, and the seesaw swings into action, with larger and faster changes on the other side of the pivot.

Learning new techniques for ourselves is the first step for making change happen. If we continue to do what we've done before, what makes us think the results will be any different from what we've gotten in the past? If we want new things to happen, if we want to see change around us, if we want to lead those changes, we need to do things differently.

Question three: Do people like change?

Again I ask my audience for a show of hands regarding their opinion of whether people like change. Normally the "No" votes win over "Yes," which is to say that my audience feels most people do not like change. The participants comment that people in general are fearful of change, are comfortable doing what they like doing and do not want to try new things, or that they are suspicious of others who may try to influence how they run their lives.

To develop this theme a bit more, I ask them to share their experiences with joyful and rewarding hobbies, tasks or activities. People then tell about their fun with golf, volunteer work, playing an instrument, and doing major projects or other pastimes that have captured their passion. As a follow-up question, I then ask them what would be their reaction to an expert offering to help them with these skills, showing them the *tips of the trade*, the special way to hold the golf club to make the perfect shot, or the way to improve their sound when playing their favorite instrument. All respond with a positive "Please give me that help!"

I then explain that they have now asked to be changed. They have in fact asked for someone to help them modify how they currently do something in order to be able to do that activity with more precision, effectiveness, beauty or skill. They want change. They like change. So what is the difference between wanting change versus not wanting change?

I suggest that the issue is the difference between *wanting* to be changed (getting *desired help*) versus being *made* to change (being *told* to do something differently). If we perceive that someone can help us to do what we want to do in a better way, then we are eager to invest in changing what we are now doing. It may turn out that we try the expert's technique and it does not automatically give us the results we expected, and we may soon revert to our old way of doing things. At first a new method feels clumsy or awkward, and does not give immediate results. We either persist and work at changing our habit until the new technique is better than the old one, or we give up and do it our old way, waiting for another new approach. In either case, our receptiveness to change at the start was open, and we were willing and ready to modify our behavior.

However, if someone just tells us we have to change our ways, we will likely feel imposed upon, skeptical or resistant to this advisor's directives. Thus, the path to being the change maker (the leader who has the job of modifying the behavior of the others), is to find the way to show the others that this proposed change is a help rather than a mandate.

The more we understand the motivations and interests of those we wish to influence, the better will be our chances of having a successful discussion. We can explain to them why and how they will be better served to make the changes that we feel are necessary. With good communications, utilizing feedback and honest dialogue and listening, the leader is more likely to create a sense of help rather than a sense of harm.

We all know that at times there really is no choice. A new corporate policy or procedure has been established, or a new rule at home must be followed, and our job is to implement the change and get all to follow the new behavior. We do not have the luxury to listen and respond to all the reasons why it is inconvenient to make the change and how it would be best to just keep things the way they are.

However, as a leader, your success with these situations is best served to the degree that you can at least appeal to the understanding of the others in your group. If they can see the issue as clearly as the decision makers who require the change, then perhaps your team will also see the benefits of compliance (survival of the company, keeping their heads above water when the bills pile up and income is down, or just keeping their jobs by following the rules). Understanding the benefit and consequences of making a change (or defying the change) can increase the potential for supportive behaviors instead of resistive behaviors.

This transition chapter had one purpose: to crystallize the concepts that (1) people who make change happen get rewards, (2) to be a change maker you must first begin thinking about what you need to change in yourself, and (3) people don't want to *be changed* but may indeed want to change for their own improvement. Changing yourself does not imply that you now are doing something bad or wrong, it just means that there may be techniques that are more effective and productive. Refinement is change. Shifting that fulcrum closer to you, by learning and practicing new techniques, is the refinement and mental conditioning that can bring success. It's that one slice at a time. You can do it, and reap the rewards!

The power of positive reinforcement

As a leader, you may often face team members who are slow or unwilling to change, to modify their habits, or they just don't want to try a new approach. In the next chapter, we will look more closely at why people do what they do, and how you can be more effective at influencing the needed changes in their behaviors. Learn to lead the change process through the power of positive reinforcement. Please read on.

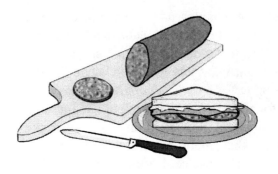

Chapter 6

The Power of Positive Reinforcement

Are they nuts?

Do you ever wonder why people do odd things? Have you ever had a boss, subordinate, friend or family member that just seemed to be in another world, or did things that test your patience? He or she behaves in ways that make you wonder:

"What is he thinking?"

"Why did she do that?"

"Why can't he change?"

Their behaviors can range from annoying to destructive, or from counterproductive to what just seems nutty. Speaking of which, I recently received one of those Internet stories that relates to what we're about to cover in this chapter. It came to me entitled "A Test For Mental Patients."

It doesn't hurt to take a hard look at yourself from time to time. This little test should get you started.

During a visit to the mental asylum, a visitor asked the Director what is the criterion that defines whether a patient should be institutionalized.

"Well," said the Director, "we fill up a bathtub; we offer a teaspoon, a teacup and a bucket to the patient and ask the patient to empty the bathtub."

1. *Would the patient use the spoon?*

2. *Would the patient use the teacup?*

3. *Would the patient use the bucket?*

"Oh, I understand," said the visitor, "A normal person would choose the bucket as it is larger than the spoon."

"No," answered the Director. "A normal person would pull the plug."

Did you pass?

Okay, this is not a real test, but another trick question. However, this story lets us think about how people approach problem solving, or do what they do in ways that appear curious or downright strange to us. In any case, we're not going to explore the world of the insane in this chapter, but we are going to review why the behavior of others may seem nuts when you want them to do one thing and they do anything but what you hope for. Do you find yourself feeling as though you are asking others to empty the tub and they begin the task with the teaspoon rather than pull the plug?

It's all about consequences

Why do people do what they do? Behavioral scientists tell us that our behavior is shaped by consequences. To better understand this we need to talk a bit about actions or events that motivate us to behave in one way or another. For example, why do we go see a particular movie? What influences our choice and action?

On one hand, there are influences that occur prior to our behavior, before we have made the choice to go to a specific movie. On the other hand, there are influences that occur after we do something, such as our reactions to a movie we have just seen. Those who write books about behavioral science speak about antecedents (actions or events that occur before a behavior) and consequences (events that are produced by the behavior and occur during or after the behavior is performed). They explain that the behavioral model is based on consequences as the reason why we repeat behaviors and do what we do. For an excellent resource to understand behavior I suggest you read "Other People's Habits – How to use positive reinforcement to bring out the best in people around you" by Aubrey C. Daniels.

I might put the explanation in less technical terms as follows: We do what we do because of what happens when we do it. As one jokester put it, "Hard work pays off in the future. Laziness pays off now." The "pay off" is the reinforcement, and that's what builds behavior patterns and habits, good or bad. Related to the joke, timing of the pay off also influences the strength of the reinforcement, and we will also discuss that issue later in this chapter.

Let's use our "going to the movie" example to become familiar with the terms and to see what really drives our behavior. Eventually we will use this wisdom and understanding to get the bathtub emptied by people pulling the plug rather than selecting the spoon!

What influences exist in our environment that may prompt the decision to go to the movies or to see a particular movie? It may be advertisements that appear and peak our curiosity. It may be a recommendation of a friend that this is a *must see* movie. Maybe we just want to do something different to relax. These influences are all called antecedents, as they are influences prior to the behavior of going to the movie. Antecedents influence behavior one time. They are prompts that get us to do something or try something.

The question of whether we will repeat the behavior, or whether the behavior eventually becomes a habit, in our example to go back to the movies again, or go back to see that style of movie, depends on the consequences. How we felt after seeing that movie determines whether we would want to repeat that behavior. Did the movie relax us, as we wanted? Did the movie have too much blood and violence for our taste? Did the movie make us feel good? Did we laugh until we cried? The answers to these questions, for the individual, are what determine that individual's behavior the next time, and the time after that, related to repeating the movie-going behavior (or the behavior to go again to see that particular kind of movie or the particular stars in the movie).

The clue is to understand that consequences dictate the likelihood of behavior being repeated. If we feel good about the consequences, we will do the behavior again. If the consequences are disagreeable, we will probably avoid that behavior the next time. How does this all tie into good leadership techniques and emptying the bathtub?

Positive and negative reinforcement of behavior

The "Slice the Salami" model for successful change is based on this concept of positive consequences. Eating the sandwich (making small changes) tastes good, offers desirable consequences (you feel good and you don't choke on the whole salami), and encourages you to repeat the behavior. You take another bite of the sandwich, and you prepare another sandwich when hungry. Eventually the pleasant behavior, or habit of eating the sandwich when hungry, takes hold and before you know it, the whole salami has been consumed. Continued reinforcement, repetition of the favorable consequence, strengthens the behavioral pattern.

A consequence perceived as positive, or favorable, is referred to as "positive reinforcement." As a result of positive reinforcement, the favorable consequences of the particular behavior, the new behavior seems more comfortable (is more rewarding) and you continue to repeat the behavior. You have adjusted to the new behavior and seek more of it.

Of course, negative consequences also shape future behavior. As a leader, it is important to understand what behaviors are most likely to repeat depending on the reinforcement you provide, either positive or negative.

Let's consider another example of modifying behavior through either negative or positive reinforcement. Let's imagine that you are the boss, and you hold a routine weekly staff meeting. You hope these meetings will be an important part of staff coordination and communication for constructive and productive use of everyone's time. Unfortunately, let's imagine that one of your workers, let's call him Joe, habitually comes to the meeting late. You'd like him to change his behavior.

One way is **through negative reinforcement:** Joe's tardiness results in consequences that are negative to him. He is scolded in front of his peers, he is made to feel bad for his action, or he is punished in some way. The behavioral scientists tell us, and we know from our own experience, that individuals normally modify behavior **just enough to avoid the punishment**. But they modify their behavior no further than necessary to avoid the negative consequences. This means, for this example, that Joe will arrange his schedule and modify his behavior just enough to arrive close enough to the correct time, to avoid being scolded or embarrassed, but no further. He will not get there any earlier, he will just be sure to not be too late. What if we try positive reinforcement?

There is another relevant term called shaping. This means giving positive reinforcement whenever we see movement towards the ultimate objective. Small (sandwich) steps in the right direction get rewarded. In our example with Joe, let's first assume we have privately asked him to try to get to the meetings on time. We might have a conversation with Joe similar to this: *"Joe, every time you arrive late at the meeting, you are effectively wasting the company's money as the rest of the group sits idle until we start the meeting. In addition, your behavior is discourteous to your peers and to me. We have all made the effort to get to the meeting room on time, and your delay wastes our time. We could start on time, whether you are there or not, but then you miss important issues that are the essence and purpose of the meeting. Accordingly, I am asking you to make the effort to plan ahead, and show your peers and me that you can do what is necessary to attend on time."*

Then if Joe is still late, but less late, we could say something constructive about his effort to arrive earlier. Assuming that Joe appreciates the praise and your public acknowledgement of his effort, this positive reinforcement of his modified behavior is more likely to increase Joe's motivation to hear repeat praise and in turn generate his interest to try to arrive earlier at the next meeting. Eventually Joe will be on time.

However, (and this is an important distinction between positive and negative reinforcement) **with positive reinforcement the discretionary effort of the individual is not limited.** Joe will be more likely not only to arrive on time, but with proper reinforcement will potentially arrive early, perhaps then become the first to be there and he will begin to be a more constructive contributor to all of the meetings. His positive reward for proper behavior will stimulate repetition of the better behaviors. His potential is limitless, rather than only improving to the point of no punishment.

A similar example can be provided for a household situation. Perhaps a child goes out with friends and continues to return home later than promised (like coming late to the worksite meeting). As a parent, the household leader, the degree to which a consistent system of rewards, punishment, consequences, praise and prodding are all used will generate the behavior changes you are seeking. Shaping behavior with positive reinforcement would typically give you the most significant swing in favorable behavior.

Coaching to success

Perhaps the most obvious area where shaping shows results is in the context of any skill that can be coached to success. In my own experience as a gymnast and coach of gymnastics I've had decades of first-hand exposure to improving difficult skills with a learning process that addresses minuscule corrections, one at a time. A new gymnast does not learn to flip his or her body upside down on the first try. There are various obstacles to overcome, including fear, strength, flexibility, timing and the application of physics to launch a body into the air and then to land correctly.

A good coach looks at what is not right, and picks the one or two most critical things to correct first. A novice gymnast feels almost blind as he or she spins through the air for the first time. It is difficult to know up from down, when to tuck tighter, when to open and be ready for the landing. The coach must give that critical feedback.

A bad coach, on the other hand, might give too much feedback, expecting the beginner to correct a dozen errors at once. This is overwhelming. The shaping must be tailored to the skill level and awareness of the recipient, to assure that he or she can understand and act upon the input. In addition, the bad coach might yell and scream with negative feedback, which will not get optimum results from the athlete.

Similarly, if any of you have learned how to play an instrument, you have likely been the recipient of shaping as well. Your teacher probably told you when you were improving in your finger or mouth positions (for string or wind instruments) to help you gradually refine your technique.

These are all examples of shaping behavior. The same process works for the work and home environments: focus on the most important next skill to refine, and then give positive feedback when the person shows improvement.

All in the eyes of the recipient

A word of caution is needed here. The concept of positive reinforcement is always, I repeat always, in the eyes of the recipient. What makes the **recipient** feel better, more positive, is what counts, not what you think should be more positive.

Some people thrive on public recognition. Others are shy and prefer not to be singled out in front of their peers. Some hate to be highlighted as rule-breakers or meeting disrupters, and others thrive on this attention to show their uniqueness. If you don't understand what the person feels as positive or negative, your good intentions may inadvertently generate behaviors quite different from your objective and aspirations.

The definition of positive reinforcement is that action or consequence that follows a behavior, which increases the repetition of that behavior. However, **the perception of positive is always from the point of view of the individual whose behavior is being modified.** Whatever it is that causes the behavior to repeat is a positive reinforcement.

Good leaders tune in to the reactions that their comments create. These leaders learn to distinguish between consequences that generate repeated behaviors that are desirable from those consequences that yield undesirable results. Refinement of consequences to refine behaviors becomes one of the ways that top leaders get more results that are favorable, quicker and more productive.

These leaders have learned to read their team members and modify their own communication of rewards in ways that most effectively bring about individual and group behavior changes and the desired repeat behaviors. These leaders use positive reinforcement to bring out the best in people around them.

Timing is critical

When is the best time to offer the positive reinforcement? The answer: when the behavior is happening. When kids at home are playing well together, that is the best time for parents to say something about it to the kids. Often, the parents don't want to interrupt the tranquility of the moment. However, they are really missing the opportunity to positively reinforce the behavior they want to see repeated.

When a supervisor comes across two employees who are normally at odds, working together in harmony, this is the best time to comment and reinforce the cooperation. When a maintenance supervisor observes a worker doing a task safely (wearing personal protective gear, properly isolating the work space to prevent risks to others, properly anticipating potential hazards and demonstrating corrective preventive actions), that is the perfect time to make a comment. When the driver of a car sees passengers buckle-up their seat belts, that is the time to thank them for their safety awareness.

However, don't just assume that the good habits will continue. They need refueling.

In fact, the author of the book, "Other People's Habits," Aubrey C. Daniels, uses the analogy of reinforcement as fuel. Without the fuel of positive reinforcement, the behavior finally dies. Extinction is the behavioral term. Without reinforcement, the new or proper behavior will become extinct, as happened to the dinosaurs, and habits drift back to old ways.

Reinforce desired behaviors to prevent extinction.

Remember to apply the slice the salami concept. Movement in the right direction needs reinforcement in small continuous bites, since the ability to make a giant leap may be unlikely or impossible at first, as if the person tried to eat the whole salami. Each successive step in the right direction, when reinforced, will promote continued behavior modification in the right direction, leading to your ultimate goal. Catch people in the act of doing things right, and say something about it that is perceived as positive to them. And keep doing it. We all need the nourishment of continuous fuel, positive reinforcement, steady bites of the sandwich, to keep on functioning.

Keep these key points in mind as you work to build a unified team, with all your group, family or friends pulling in the same direction:

- To reinforce behavior that you want to see happen again, reward the behavior when it is happening.

- Reward can be simply acknowledging your awareness of the person's activity with some positive comment, a smile or praise (being sensitive to what the person perceives as positive to them).

- If someone's behavior is far from what you want, begin to *shape* this person's progress in the right direction with positive reinforcement as movement gets closer to what you want, and continue to do so as the person continues to get closer to the objective.

- It takes many repetitions of reinforcement to change behavior and to have it stick. Failure to have further reinforcement will eventually lead to extinction of the desired behavior.

With this in mind, we can now return to the bathtub project. "Why are those nuts using a teaspoon?" you may ask yourself, as you watch others do a task inappropriately. But first ask yourself whether you gave them the big picture well enough. Do they share your perspective? Did you explain the objectives clearly? Why are they doing the task that way, and what have you done to signal them about your expectations?

What reinforcement are you giving them when they either continue to use the spoon (are you ignoring or chastising?), or when you see them considering other options (are you acknowledging their use of more productive problem solving techniques)? Their behaviors, their habits, are influenced by your behavior, that is to say your reactions to their behavior. The consequences of their behavior, established by you, dictate whether their favorable behaviors will continue and whether their unfavorable behaviors will change. You can change people's habits when you first take a hard look at your own habits for constructive use of positive reinforcement.

From studying the work of behavioral scientists, to watching other successful leaders at work, there is a lot to learn about how to improve your odds at getting better results. In fact, your life should be a continual process of learning. That's our focus for the next chapter.

Chapter 7

Continuous Learning

Why should you keep learning, and how can you get the training you need?

So you want to advance in your career, right? How will you learn the key skills necessary for success in that next great job? Will you be ready when the perfect job opportunity surfaces? How do you get ready? Or are you now at home, and are concerned that you have lost touch with some of the skills needed for the business world? What can you do to get up to speed?

Career entry and advancement normally means taking on new responsibilities and thus using new skills. Typically, each higher level of responsibility requires the application of new abilities.

For example, when you work as an individual contributor you don't normally have to exercise control over subordinates, whereas when you are a department head this skill becomes one of your major factors for success. Similarly, multi-department responsibility requires a mix of other capabilities such as planning, strategic vision, budgeting, control of spending versus a budget, or familiarity with diverse and specialized disciplines such as sales, accounting, marketing, engineering, or other unique and perhaps greatly different functions than those you are using in your current job, or have used in past work experience.

When a position is vacant and the boss is looking to select the best candidate for this spot, the boss would love to have a person who can jump right in and handle the key job requirements. Thus, the basis for screening of candidates for job openings is their prior experience with the skills needed to succeed in the proposed position. Accordingly, as you plot your future job options, you must begin with an assessment of the likely skills that will be needed for that next best opportunity. Then, start to learn these skills!

If you have never had the chance to build a budget from the ground up, or never had to be in charge of several other individuals to get a task done, or if you have never made a sales call, and you want to gain these experiences, how do you start to learn what's needed? Where can you build your base of experience?

Who will provide you with special skills training?

Too often, we expect the company to provide special training seminars, to send us off to charm school, or to provide classes that will help us to learn skills necessary for our next promotion or new job responsibility. The sad truth is *don't hold your breath waiting for the company gift!*

I worked for 40 years in a commodity industry, where product value could swing from $1,000 per ton to less than $100 per ton in only a few months, depending on the competitive global market. In addition, the business ran through annual cycles where some years we did quite well, and programs such as training and development were reinstated, but during other years we had all we could do just to survive. During the tight times, headcount was cut, programs were slashed and some fringe benefits disappeared.

Training and development programs often suffer from these economic challenges.

Unfortunately, whether you are in a commodity business too, or part of a fast growing sector, you cannot simply rely on your company to provide you with the skills you will need for your future (either with your current employer, or with another company). You should establish a self-development action plan that allows you to continually expand your knowledge base, learn new skills and gain new experiences that will not only be interesting to you as you learn, but will serve you for future fortune. Of course, if you are at home, not currently employed, then there is no "company" to offer training in any case. The approach to your own development may nonetheless follow a path similar to those in the business world.

Learn for free

One of the best ways to advance your skills is to volunteer, and it's free. This volunteerism can be within your own company or completely independent of your work world. Let's take these options one at a time.

Within your company, you can insert yourself into the precise experiences you are seeking. If possible, this is your best first approach, since it not only connects you to the particular skills and jargon appropriate for your business and company, but also connects you to key leaders with influence in the company structure. Inside the company, assignments can be done in a formal way through your company's annual goal setting program, or they can be done as a more informal initiative on your own.

Volunteer as part of your annual goal-setting process

Most annual performance reviews consist of a look back and a look forward. The supervisor reviews your past performance against goals and analyzes your successes, as well as identifies areas for improvement. Ultimately, your accomplishments are tied to salary and benefits. Accordingly, you want to excel in this annual review. Similarly, this is generally the time to establish your goals for the coming year. You are now in the perfect position to have a serious chat with your supervisor about your future, and how you can best prepare for new opportunities.

Aside from the typical current job-function goals, with job-specific tasks to accomplish in the coming twelve months, your annual goals should also include a few tasks focused on your growth and development. For example, if your past experience did not yet allow you the chance to build a budget, then this is your moment to ask for the opportunity. At first, it may be to ask your boss to let you help assemble data for the coming year's budget, or to work with the whole budget planning process as the company proceeds through the cycle. Be creative with your boss. Ask what the boss thinks is the best way to learn, and the most appropriate way to get you involved.

Why is this goal-setting technique a good way to get started? Because, it provides a formal way for you and your boss to focus on your skill development within the company. Through the year, using this budgeting example, you and your boss can work together in broadening your exposure to accounting systems, control systems, the nuts and bolts of how a budget is constructed, how it is defended and how you can sell the budget to those who have approval authority. Each of these experiences and skills will serve you in your path towards budget familiarity.

Perhaps a year later you can include a follow-up goal to be in charge of a larger part of the budget process, or overall responsibility for budget assembly for your supervisor. Think about how you can help your supervisor with this task, increasing responsibility as time goes on, and learning all along the way. You help the boss and you help yourself. A win-win! What boss would not like to get that excellent help?

Another advantage of the annual goal-setting process as your way to skill development is that it documents your success with your new abilities. Aside from gaining exposure to new skills and learning new disciplines, you have a track-record that becomes part of the company record in the next year-end performance review. You and your boss will be sitting down again to discuss your progress, and your new budget skill (or any other specialty you agree to include) will be recognized and recorded. This helps reinforce your growth and sets you up for more exposure within the company.

Even though budgeting is not part of your official job responsibility, you will be seen within the company as a person who has been involved in the process. People from accounting, finance, and other departments who attend the same meetings will know about your involvement and capability.

Don't be afraid to ask

In sales, there's an expression "If you don't ask, you don't get." The meaning is clear, namely that you should not be afraid to ask for something that you want or need. There's normally no harm in asking. Just don't be a nag.

Accordingly, when you and your supervisor are formally talking about your career development and your goals for the coming year, this might be the best time to ask about the company supporting you in a program such as Menttium. As you can see by searching their website on the Internet, Menttium offers an excellent program where mid-career professionals are paired with an external, out-of-their-company mentor for a yearlong process of coaching and skills refinement.

I have had the honor to be one of these external volunteer mentors for over a decade, and can assure you that the process provides an outstanding opportunity for you to have a personal mentor, similar to having a personal trainer for your work environment. This experience can bring you to a new level in your career ladder through leadership awareness and job-specific techniques that can work for you. Even as a mentor, you can gain new skills and perspectives that can help you in your career. Consider volunteering on this side of the process with Menttium, as a mentor, especially if you are more advanced in your career.

Who knows, if your company is in a profit cycle that allows financial support for such external programs, and if your needs coincide with the profile for what Menttium believes would be matched best with my background, then I might even become your personal mentor for a year! If however your company is in a down cycle of profit, then at least inquire about internal mentor-mentee matches, to see if you can be part of such a program.

A development tool for your family or work team

Also in the spirit of "Don't be afraid to ask" (if you don't ask, you don't get), I too will ask: Why not order several more of these books to serve as continuous learning opportunities for members of your family and your work team? All can develop in place, finding tips that work for them as I hope they work for you. As you all refine techniques together, the rate of change for improvements accelerates. You benefit, they benefit and, of course, I will enjoy knowing more people are learning tips from my book that will help them to become more successful.

Now, let's get back to you, and how you can employ additional techniques for continuous learning.

An informal approach within the company works too

Aside from the formal annual goal process, you can begin volunteer learning initiatives on your own. You don't need your boss to approve this (unless your boss is a real micromanager control type!) and you don't need to have a formal documentation program either. Just go out and seek the learning opportunities yourself.

Back when I was in manufacturing, I realized that my future career growth could be enhanced by exposure to the sales side of the company, by gaining more business knowledge. I had my Master's in administration, had been a plant manager in various locations, and did lots of internal sales with programs such as safety, cost control and environmental responsibility. However, to that point in my career I had not yet had direct exposure with customers other than when they visited our plant to see where their purchased products originated.

So I simply asked one of the sales representatives if I could accompany him on a sales call sometime. Our *excuse* for me to join him on such a call was that as the plant manager, it was a way for me to understand the customer's needs better. By seeing the customer's facility first-hand, and hearing from his or her own lips what needs were critical I would be able to provide better service to the customer when I returned to my plant. It helped the sales representative too, by allowing him to show special concern for the customer by adding more depth of support during the customer visit.

For me, it was a great first-look at the other side of our company. This visit immediately and irrevocably broadened my horizons. Years later, with a half billion dollars per year of international sales responsibility, as a senior vice president of our company, my growth had perhaps been best served by this simple first step.

Look at the people around you. Where are the experts in your organization and what are the tasks that they are doing that you need to learn? Who has the best record of accomplishment in specific skills? How might all of these in-house experts help you?

Imagine yourself walking into the office of one of your company's leaders in a particular discipline that you want to learn about. You can initiate a conversation to discuss opportunities with comments that may include any of these questions that fit your circumstances: *"I am trying to look ahead at my career to discover areas of our company where my current exposure and skills are lacking. I see you as one of the leading examples of a person who knows how to do this function well. Would you mind sharing with me some time or providing direction to me about how I might gain some informal exposure to your discipline? How can I learn about your area? What books would you suggest I read (what are your favorites)? How did you get interested in this field yourself? How did you make a transition to it from another area of expertise? What else would you suggest that I consider, in order to learn more? I'd even be willing to do some volunteer tasks working with you and your team, just so I could get some exposure. What would you suggest?"*

You never know. Your whole career might hinge on making that first step across the threshold of an expert's door, in an area where you know little but he or she knows a lot. Ask for this potential mentor's help, and ask to volunteer. This informal in-company approach, aside from the formal annual goal setting process, can expand your education and opportunities greatly.

Think of at-work continuous learning as a self-directed MBA program

Often students complain that the courses in school have no relevance to their future real-world requirements. However, you can view these self-initiated volunteer development experiences as a home-made MBA program (where MBA can now stand for *"My Business Advancement"*). This is your opportunity to mold a set of "classes" that are 100% applicable to what you need to learn. Every detail is relevant. In fact, this initiative can be a way to spice-up an otherwise dull patch in your work.

Create your own MBA course: My Business Advancement.

I mentored a friend working in New Zealand who was not sure of his future direction. He was torn between leaving the corporate sector, and either working for himself or for a not-for-profit organization. His work, though interesting, was becoming routine and was no longer exciting for him.

I suggested that he begin thinking about the skills that he needs to learn for whatever he might next pursue. What kinds of experiences has he yet to master? What next-step demands will be placed on him, either working for himself, a non-profit or a major corporation? In what areas of his development does he need the chance to gain training and experience?

I suggested that he look within his company to find mentors willing to help him get exposure to these skills, and thereby start to build his experience base. Each new skill could be looked at as another course to take, working towards his own MBA curriculum.

He was immediately enthused. He had not considered this approach, and was eager to make his list of development needs, and then to seek opportunities in his current work environment to explore these. Suddenly, his work took on a new fresh feel, with every day being a rejuvenating chance to see and learn more. You can do this too, enjoying new things to learn while building a stronger résumé.

You can make use of your company's formal goal process to get experience, get exposure and get skills that you need for future job advancement, or you can make use of other in-company techniques you initiate informally. In addition, you can make use of non-work opportunities. Of course, this non-work approach directly applies to those currently away from a corporate environment, since they do not have access to business functions and departments.

Outside the company there are additional ways to learn and grow

Think about your personal life outside the work environment. Do you belong to a club, a religious group, a community group, or other social cluster? Most of these organizations typically offer great volunteer learning opportunities. They desperately need help, and are willing to let almost anyone who wants to contribute to get involved. Moreover, you learn while doing. In addition, failure is tolerated more easily! There are no formal performance reviews that impact annual salary compensation. The group does not "look a gift horse in the mouth." Of course, they want capable help, but are generally sympathetic to the volunteer's learning curve. It is a nice way to break in to new experiences and skills.

Using the same budgeting example from above, think about your local associations and those that have budgets to forecast and manage their limited funds. Someone is probably doing that function now and you could ask this person if your help would be allowed. Allow you to help? This person will probably dance with joy to get your help! You can begin with this volunteer explaining the budget process to you. Then you could ask to do particular parts to assist. Finally, you could volunteer some more with taking on as much responsibility as you can for this task. Whether it is a multi-million dollar corporation or a small community group, the basics of accounting, responsibility and coordination will be common to each. Both organizations will share many of the same needs and techniques. In fact, often a local group has a highly qualified corporate accounting person doing this volunteer role anyway, thus it is as though you are getting your own professional tutor free!

You will learn new skills, terminology and techniques, as well as discover potential problems and how to resolve them. Over time, you will find you are no longer a novice in budgeting, or in other skills such as group leadership, or in making cold-call sales, or in planning large functions (project management) or in any one of a number of skills that directly translate to the corporate life. Your skill sets increase in direct proportion to your creativity and willingness to volunteer. After doing this off-work exposure, you may feel more confident to explore similar in-company opportunities. In any case, your résumé can reflect your non-work experiences and skills as well as your work related history, and this may increase your odds to pass the screening process when job applicants are being considered for a vacancy.

To learn best, do it!

The volunteer role, to actually do things, is the best way to gain and retain your skills needed for your future. You can read about the tasks, talk to others about what you need to do or watch others at work doing these skills. None of these methods will stick with you as much as rolling up your sleeves and trying them for yourself. That is how you learn fastest and remember for the long term.

Why do more than just read about new techniques, or simply watch skilled experts do their jobs? My answer to you reminds me of a conversation I had during my first days on a real job after college. As a new engineer, I had a senior engineer mentor in the company named Paul Yoon. Paul was from Korea and he shared a saying from his home country with me that had to do with learning. He said the expression roughly translated to English is *"Learn easy, forget easy. Learn hard, remember always."* Or, simply stated, if things are too easy when you first face them, they do not stick with you as long as those experiences where you have to work hard at the task to achieve the result. We learn *long* from those memorable efforts.

You also recall from Chapter 2, dealing with effective communications, I referred to the Trump-Kiyosaki book and the "Cone of Learning" study. This is where they described that we learn most and retain longest those experiences that stem from active involvement (doing, simulating and participating in an activity) rather than from passive involvement (watching, listening or reading). Thus, if you are trying to develop new skills for your future it is best to supplement *passive* input with *active* opportunities to learn. Your volunteer effort to do the tasks will provide an ideal path to long-term development of the desired skills.

Having trouble finding areas where you may volunteer?

Check the Internet. You can search in your area for organizations that need volunteer help. Talk to their directors. Find the opportunities you are looking for to help others and to help yourself. There are also books on the topic of how to develop yourself. For example, Michael M. Lombardo and Robert W. Eichinger have written "Eighty-eight Assignments for Development in Place," providing a wide range of examples from small projects and start-ups to off-job activities which can enhance your professional or personal experiences.

Speaking of the Internet, this related item from the Internet caught my attention and I hope you find it helpful as well.

"In a university commencement address several years ago, Brian Dyson, CEO of Coca Cola Enterprises, spoke of the relation of work to one's other commitments:

Imagine life as a game in which you are juggling five balls in the air. You name them – work, family, health, friends and spirit – and you're keeping all of these in the air. You will soon understand that work is a rubber ball. If you drop it, it will bounce back. But the other four balls – family, health, friends and spirit – are made of glass. If you drop one of these, they will be irrevocably scuffed, marked, nicked, damaged or even shattered. They will never be the same. You must understand that and strive for balance in your life. How do you do this?" Among Brian Dyson's multiple tips, he included this one that relates to our topic: *"Don't be afraid to learn. Knowledge is weightless, a treasure you can always carry easily."*

In other words, what you learn today you can always use. The process of learning not only prepares you for particular skills needed for promotion and career growth, but also serves you in life overall. We are sometimes surprised at how one skill or fact originally learned to serve us in one way may find itself useful again for many other purposes. Enjoy the pleasure of learning throughout life, and let it help you make the most of yours.

Some basic advice about continuous learning

Regardless of where you are in your life-cycle, such as a new college graduate starting out in a career, a mid-level manager looking to grow in your company, an at-home person thinking about re-joining the commercial world, or anyone who simply enjoys the process of finding new interests and experiences, the underlying message throughout all of this chapter is to keep learning. Learning enriches your life and broadens your opportunities.

I am lucky to have a good friend, John Guy LaPlante, the world's oldest Peace Corps volunteer in 2009 (at 80), author of "Around the World at 75. Alone Dammit!" and other life adventure books. He's a good friend, and his experience and wisdom mean a lot to me. As I was writing this book, aside from John's editorial help and inspirational mentoring, he offered me input regarding continuous learning tips for my readers. He suggested, "It might be well to remind people that just as it's essential nowadays to know how to drive, learn how to type with 10 fingers, how to become savvy with several basic computer programs, learn the basics of accounting, read a good book on modern etiquette (including telephone and e-mail etiquette), and make sure to read 'How to Make Friends and Influence People'..." He went on to suggest reading other books of this type in order to keep on growing and learning. John is the role model for such behavior with his around-the-world trips, Peace Corps volunteerism, and caring attitude.

Wherever you are in your life, seek knowledge. It's fun, it's beneficial, and it's rewarding.

Pat yourself on your back!

The fact that you are reading this book confirms your own interest in continuous learning. This self-help initiative reflects your desire to grow, refine skills, understand new concepts and try new behaviors that might improve the quality of your life and accelerate your career success. Congratulations! You demonstrate that you have the right stuff for leadership and life-long learning. Keep it up!

Skills build with time

You don't have to conquer Rome in a day. Remember to slice that salami! Begin with any next-step skill that you need to develop. Pick one and work on it, within the company, formally or informally, and outside the company with local community groups. And keep learning. It should be a continuous process!

As you work with others on such tasks, you will see the importance of your role within a team, and the importance of the team itself. Teamwork often becomes the fundamental route to overall personal and group success. Let's study that further in the next chapter, "Teamwork."

Chapter 8

Teamwork

Why is teamwork important?

Because your success depends on it. Unless you work in isolation, without any dependence on others, including customers, you will gain the most success when you excel in creating and working in effective teams.

On a small scale, you and your department represent a team. Expanding this vision further, your functional discipline represents a larger team, within the structure of the overall team, your company. Additionally, though not normally considered part of your company team, your customers are also a part of your team. Customers may be internal (within the company) or external (clients who pay the bills). If you look at your customers as part of your own group, looking for ways to maximize your common achievements, you are more likely to gain longer-term successes. At home, the family is the team. The smooth functioning of this team may be the most important factor for family success.

Let's look a bit closer at teams, and how to get the most out of them, and thereby get the most out of your own efforts for productivity, success and reward.

You've probably heard the one about....

"THE BODY PARTS MEETING

One day the different parts of the body were having an argument to see which should be in charge:

The brain said, "I do all the thinking so I'm the most important and I should be in charge."

The eyes said, "I see everything and let the rest of you know where we are, so I'm the most important and I should be in charge."

The hands said, "Without me we wouldn't be able to pick anything up or move anything. So I'm the most important and I should be in charge."

The stomach said, "I turn the food we eat into energy for the rest of you. Without me, we'd starve. So I'm the most important and I should be in charge."

The legs said: "Without me we wouldn't be able to move anywhere. I'm the most important and I should be in charge."

Then the rectum said, "I think I should be in charge."

All the rest of the parts said, "YOU?!! You don't do anything! You're not as important as we are, surely! You can't be in charge!"

So the rectum closed up...

After a few days, the legs were all wobbly, the stomach was all queasy, the hands were all shaky, the eyes were all watery, and the brain was all cloudy.

They all agreed that they couldn't take any more of this and agreed to put the rectum in charge.

The moral of the story?

You don't have to be the most important to be in charge... just the rectum!"

You may have seen this story on the Internet or heard it from a friend, perhaps with an ending using cruder language. This story can also have other morals, such as it only takes one malcontent to screw up a good plan, or alternatively, someone who may seem to be a minor player may have a more important role than he or she – or anybody else – thinks.

The organization, or company, is indeed similar to a human body. It functions best as a whole, from head to foot, all parts (departments and individuals) contributing with their own unique skills, consistent with the master plan. If one part of the whole is out of synch, or working counterproductively, then it is like a cancer that can grow and destroy the whole. As a leader, or as a team member, you all have responsibility to improve teamwork. Failure of the body, means failure of the parts. Brain or rectum are useless in a dead body. Individual employees do not prosper in a failing company. Do your part to assure the whole can survive.

When you are the leader of a group, at work or at home, you have to be sensitive to each of the team members. Listen to their input, gain their insights, and respect the differences of each person. Some are shy and don't immediately share their input, some try to dominate conversations and do not offer a chance for others to chime in. A leader's role is to encourage constructive debate (this differs from bitching and complaining in that you are seeking solutions, not just venting to surface problems).

As a team member, you have a responsibility to the process too. Be careful to not monopolize the conversations. Be respectful to your peers. Help bring out others who are quiet, to encourage their input too. Help the group to refocus if needed, with occasional questions such as "What is our objective here?" or "What other way can we solve this problem?" or "What crazy ideas might we explore just to see alternatives?" Every member of a brainstorm session has a role, and any member can be the person who sparks the path to the best group solution.

I've more than once had staff members who I knew were smart and had good ideas, but their self-confidence, behavior in groups or other dynamics had them silent during problem solving meetings. I would make a point to talk to them (typically in private) and let them know that I valued their input. In fact, I needed their input. I would explain that as smart as they were, if they did not give me their ideas, then I may as well not have them in the room and not have them on my team. We are paying them to be problem solvers, which means they must add to the dynamics of group discussion, problem resolution and brainstorming. In subsequent group problem solving meetings, I would be alert to their contributions, commenting positively when they opened up. The leader's role is to get the most out of the team. Tune in to group dynamics.

It is not enough for the smart ones to go back to their rooms, in isolation, and crank out a solution for consideration by the boss. Brainstorming within a group can generate better solutions. During such a work session, one idea, for example from a smart one, may not be the ultimate solution, but it may spark another off-the-wall idea by another teammate, and in turn generate a better path to solving the problem at hand. Silence stifles solutions. Participation prompts progress.

This issue of finding better solutions through teamwork reminds me of a typical team-building exercise that perhaps you have experienced, dealing with making decisions about the priority order for emergency supplies on the moon. The ten minute exercise is done first on your own, taking only five minutes, and later with the help of other participants all trying to prioritize the list together, taking only another five minutes.

Take the ten-minute teamwork challenge.

If you have done this experiment, you can breeze through the following section. However, if you have not ever had fun with this exercise, I recommend that you and a few friends (or at least one friend or family member) grab a paper and pencil, follow the instructions below, draw your own conclusions, but do *not* check the Internet link provided below for the correct answers until appropriate.

Take ten minutes to discover something about teamwork

The challenge: Imagine you are returning to the base ship on the sunlit side of the moon after carrying out a 72-hour exploration trip. Your small spacecraft has crash-landed about 200 miles from the base ship. You need to reach the base ship. In addition to your spacesuit, you were able to salvage the items listed below. Using what you know about the moon, rate each item in the list below according to how important it would be in getting you back to the base ship.

Reorganize the items below, listing on your sheet of paper what you consider the most important first (#1) and the least important last (#15). The printed list below is *not* in the correct priority order, according to NASA, and your job is to re-sort the items.

- 4 packages of food concentrate
- 20 meters of nylon rope
- 1 portable heating unit
- 1 magnetic compass
- 1 box of matches
- 1 first-aid kit
- 2 50-kg tanks of oxygen
- 20 liters of water
- 1 star chart
- 1 case of dehydrated milk
- 1 solar-powered radio set
- 3 signal flares
- 1 large piece of insulating fabric
- 1 flashlight
- 2 45-caliber pistols, loaded

However, before jumping into the exercise, please follow these steps:

1. First, find a few friends or family members (or at least one other player) to do this exercise with you (the exercise will take only ten minutes).

2. Then, do this exercise by yourself, limiting your time to five minutes. You need only a paper and pencil, a numbered list from 1 to 15, and your imagination.

3. At the same time you are doing the exercise, have your friends and family (or the other player) independently do the same task within the same 5-minute time limit, keeping their rankings to themselves.

4. Do *not* yet check the correct answers as provided by NASA on the Internet.

5. Repeat the exercise this time as a group, with the same 5-minute time limit, and all of your ideas should be freely discussed aloud, trying to optimize your original lists by comparing notes with all the participants, sharing ideas, and refining the priority ranking to create one new team list, ranked from 1 to 15.

Stop!

Do *not* do step 6, to check Internet answers, until the team exercise has been completed.

6. Now, each of you should check your original independent #1 thorough #15 ranking with the official NASA list, and do the same with the one final list that your group developed. Record the scores for yourself, each participant and for the team.

Here is an internet link for correct answers:

Internet link: http://www.oneplusyou.com/bb/moon

There are several links for this exercise, in case you want to use another source.

There are normally several lessons learned from this exercise, regardless of how the scores turn out. Review the results of your scores when each of you worked alone and the team score resulting from the group effort. Which result provided a better score? Typically, the group result is higher than any one of the individual problem solving results. Why is this?

The team problem solving approach benefits from various perspectives. Group interaction brings different skills and life experiences to the table, often with new enlightenment that your own limited individual perspective may not generate.

If you (or any team member) got a higher score when working alone, there may be several reasons why. One might be that you or the team member could not influence the group to agree with this individual priority listing. What group dynamics were in play to have you change your mind, from your better solution, to accept a different group ranking? Or, why were you unable to have the group see the wisdom of your priority order?

The problem-solving dynamics of a group become a forum for exercising leadership and management skills such as control, effective listening skills, negotiation, group thinking versus following the strength of individual positions, and many more. As a leader, it is important to focus on this process of information exchange in order to maximize your ability to create the optimum solution to the problem at hand. Similarly, as mentioned earlier, as a group member you also share in the responsibility for group results. Each person makes a difference.

More than just problem solving

The concept of teamwork applies to more than just group problem solving. The corporate body functions best when all parts work well together, as does a family unit. This cross-functional teamwork means that as a working member of the body corporate, you must seek to strengthen these relationships for your own long-term success and that of the company, and for sustaining strong family values and plans when the context is teamwork at home.

Think about alliances, mentors, mentoring, and service. Look for the skills you need, or the skills you admire in others, and seek out opportunities to learn. Watch how others solve problems, how they succinctly present a problem or a solution, or how they pay attention when someone is talking to them. Look for body language, look for spoken language, look for written language. You have an encyclopedia of information out there in your workplace and in your community that can provide the continuous learning that was addressed in the prior chapter.

Seek out a mentor to help you with areas that can stand improvement. Offer to be a mentor to others who could benefit from your own successes and styles. Team members should always be available to help when needed, to offer constructive feedback and to be open to the feedback from others. As individuals help each other, the team overall improves, and this success cycles back to the individual members again.

As a team member, you should be alert to opportunities to help others. Although teamwork implies a two-way street, each helping the other, make it your goal to be service oriented, working to assist the others whether or not they are as generous to you as you are to them. This leads us to the "Four-to-One" rule addressed in the next chapter.

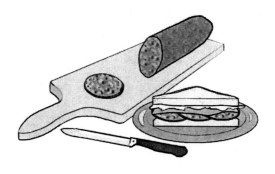

Chapter 9
The Four-to-One (4:1) Rule

Help!

This chapter is about service to others. Consider it something similar to the Golden Rule, though slightly modified:

Do unto others four times, as you would have them do unto you.

It's not actually a rule, with unbending regulations and a scorecard to track activities, but is more of a concept. Help others more often than you ask for their help. Be *service oriented*. Look for ways to be of assistance to others.

A bit of background first

Years ago when I was involved with political action in support of our company's need to obtain favorable regulatory control, I benefited from a wise and experienced expert in this field. His guidance went as follows:

"Artie, in our business we will occasionally need the help of our Local, State and Federal legislators to favorably consider how certain laws will be enacted. We will want their help and understanding. When that time comes, we want them to be well informed and receptive to our needs. Unfortunately, that is not the time to just ask for help. We first have to invest in their education, interest and good feelings about us. Before you ask for their help, you should have given them help four times over. I call it the 4:1 Rule."

Okay. Simple enough. Let the scales of assistance tip in favor of being more generous than needy. Give help more often than you ask for it. But how do you help a politician? And how can techniques to help politicians have any relevance to those of us in business who do not work with politicians, or for those of us at home?

Education and exposure

A politician has a remarkably difficult job. There are hundreds of issues with which they must deal, and most are quite complex. The first step to assisting them is providing good information about topics that are otherwise difficult to grasp. Send articles of interest. Provide briefing sheets on convoluted themes. Provide on-site explanations of your facility and programs. Be considerate of the other person's need to know, and share openly with all relevant data. Finally, the politician must make up his or her own mind and vote accordingly, but our role and objective was at least to provide them with the science and facts that we had available to us so that their decision process was as balanced as it could be.

Likewise, politicians need exposure to the public, to keep their name recognition high with issues that inspire public support. Thus, we would look for ways to get local politicians into the news, attending ribbon cutting events for projects and job expansions, being introductory speakers for a big event, and to be seen (for example, photographed by news reporters) walking through our facility talking to a worker on the floor. We'd think about ways to help the politician gain visibility and appreciation by the masses, and plan events accordingly.

By now you may be asking yourself, "So what does all this political stuff have to do with me and my job or an at home environment?" Everything!

This applies to all jobs and life situations

The concept of helping others before you ask for help is universal. It should be your Golden Rule at work and off the job as well. All of us need help from others to succeed. Accordingly, knowing that at some point we may need to ask for something (time, support, knowledge, priority), it is much better to be already postured in order for other people to feel a bit more invested in reciprocity towards you. If you've already helped them four times over, then the one time you need their help they will be more likely to provide it to you.

You need not keep score. Just be service oriented.

You don't need a score card. You need a life style of service. Even if you never have to ask for help, you will feel richer to have given even if you have not received. Most often, it costs you nothing other than some of your time or energy to share with others what might be quite valuable to them yet relatively simple for you.

Giving is an investment that pays good dividends in friendship, loyalty and commitment. As a leader, you will welcome these bonds and they will serve you and your career well. As a human being, this giving-mentality will enrich your sense of value and service independent from the context of career objectives.

Think 360 degrees

Service orientation is not just about help to politicians or customers. Better stated, consider all of your interpersonal relationships as though they all *were* with customers. You can serve them all: bosses, peers, subordinates, and clients. Look in all directions, 360°, up and down, for where and how you can help others.

We are typically oriented to serve the supervisor. Keep the boss happy and we are happy. Consequently, we may not need much time to address this concept. Simply stated, look for ways to make the job of your boss easier. What burdens can you relieve? Of course, do your job well, make targets, resolve problems.

However, you can also take initiative to see where you can pick up some of the supervisor's load. Are there tasks that you can learn and then do for the supervisor? This is a great way for succession planning and continuous learning (as discussed in the earlier chapter), and at the same time gives relief to the boss. Make the life of the boss easy, and your own life may get easier too.

For peers, the same rule applies. How can you foster cross-functional support? What can your department do to assist another? What are their needs, and what resources can you direct to give them relief? Think *support*, and open your imagination. At home, think of each family member as a peer, with needs and aspirations. Consider what you can do to ease their burdens. This extends as well to neighbors and friends.

Surprisingly, the role of service can also apply to how you work with your own subordinates. This may come as a surprise to some. In fact, most people figure that it is the role of the subordinate to serve the boss, not the other way around. Let me share a brief story that one of my subordinates told me, and which has ever since provided me with a clear vision and meaningful approach to supervision.

The track coach

One day I was chatting with one of my staff members, Tom, about leadership and supervision. We got onto the topic of roles. Tom then told me a story (that he had heard from a former boss) describing what one of the key roles of a supervisor should be.

He used the analogy of a track coach, responsible for the success of high-hurdle runners. Success is measured by the runner who gets to the finish line before all the other competitors. The similarity is not unlike the business world, where success is typically measured by the company that captures greater market share, to be first and fastest, or the department that can reach its goals fastest and consistently.

The coach wants a winning team. The runners want to be winners. They have mutual goals, as do department heads and team members in the organization (at least they should have mutual goals!). Typical roles for the coach (or boss) include teaching skills, setting targets, and providing oversight and control. However, in this story, the coach does more for the team's runners than would be allowed in the real world, but it serves the story well.

What this coach does is run out ahead of the team's sprinters during the race, and knock down each hurdle before each of the coach's runners get there, while the competitors are struggling with jumping hurdles all the way to the finish line. As a result, this team's runners do not have to waste time and energy jumping over each hurdle, and can instead make a fast dash to the finish line! What runners would not want this? They would always reach the finish line ahead of the competition.

What are you doing to knock down barriers?

Of course, this would never happen in a real race. But the image is clear: A key role of a good boss is to use the influence of power and authority to knock down burdensome barriers to the department's success. This may be in the form of modifying, streamlining or creating better company rules and procedures, or in greasing the skids for a key project with other peer or superior decision makers, or expediting approval for needed funds. The employees still have responsibility to get their jobs done, but if the boss can help make life easier, the employees can be more effective, productive and successful. The employees, boss and company win!

I have kept this image in mind ever since that conversation, and routinely looked for ways to stay out in front of my team members, to knock down obstacles that might get in their way. As bosses, we can help our subordinates by giving them skills, coaching them to success, working with their career plans, mentoring them, giving them constructive feedback, and also doing the difficult work of getting rid of wasteful corporate policies and similar burdens that needlessly obstruct work rather than enhance it.

For clients and customers (the paying kind), we similarly should look for ways to serve. Other than the basics of providing the product or service at highest possible quality for lowest possible cost, there are many soft issues that can serve the 4:1 rule as well. Be generous with communication, keeping customers aware of industry trends and technology that can help them in their own business. Share safety and environmental program tips. Every company has to deal with this important issue, and if we can help our customers to be more successful, they will appreciate such assistance. Once you begin with a *service orientation*, you will discover that there are many dimensions to your ability to help others.

Spread the sunshine

Sometimes *help* is just making the other person's day brighter. Simple courtesies, such as remembering a birthday or anniversary, or asking about a child's progress with a project or hobby, will open lines of communication and feelings of support. The best way to deliver this help is face-to-face. Being visible, being seen and seeing others, is the topic for the next chapter.

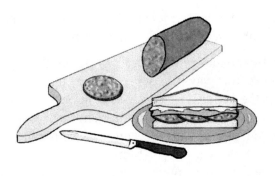

Chapter 10
Visibility

It's more than Management by Walking Around (MBWA)!

You probably have heard the philosophical question *"If a tree falls down in the woods and no one is around to hear it- does it make a sound?"*

Perhaps a work equivalent could be something such as: *"If managers are not visible to their teams or customers, will these leaders make a difference?"*

This is not to say that you can not have success if you work in the background, but instead that your visibility may be the most effective way to make change happen. A major part of doing a good job is connecting with your people. You need to get out from behind the desk and meet face-to-face with your personnel and your clients.

There are many good reasons for this personal interaction, which I will address in this chapter, but it is more than just the *walking around* that produces results. In this chapter, you will learn what to look for, how to react, and how to plan your encounters for greatest return on your investment of time while you are out there, away from your desk.

Making a difference

A great satisfaction in my career was the opportunity to make a difference. Many of my assignments were to accept challenging tasks where culture change was needed, with rapid correction of faulty safety programs, poor environmental records, unacceptable financial performance and lack of team morale. My job was to fix the problems quickly. When you work hard to make a difference, and see the fruits of your efforts, there is a wonderful sense of accomplishment. In my case, it is pleasing to think back about achievements such as the following:

- Managing a plant that had one of the worst safety records in the corporation, and then reducing injuries to one quarter of the prior record performance. Creating a dramatic culture change also cut environmental incidents in half and slashed SARA environmental emissions (USA Federal Government Standards) by 25% from prior years.

- Turning around a non-profitable business, which had seven prior consecutive years of losses, to a profitable unit with 40% year-over-year income growth. Establishing a "mean-shift" in safety performance for the North American operations, meaning that there was a "statistically significant" change in average performance, not just luck or a short-term trend. Actual results demonstrated nearly a ten-fold reduction in injuries, which ultimately allowed us to receive our corporation's highest honor for environmental excellence, two consecutive years, given to only one plant site annually in our company's world-wide operations.

- Receiving the corporation's highest Profit Improvement Program award two years in a row, despite moving from one plant to another (after winning the global award at one site, I was assigned to another plant and within a year that plant was the corporate leader).

- At a 2,400 person union site where I began my career, a newly developed preventive maintenance program cut motor failures in half, and a 5-year capital reliability improvement program increased on-stream time for the process units.

Of course, there are many factors that contribute to successful statistics, but one element that consistently provided me with favorable results was the face-to-face delivery of my vision, commitment and passion for excellence. This does not happen through bulletin board notices from the department head, plant manager or senior vice president. This comes from the department head, plant manager or senior vice president talking to people, listening to their concerns and aspirations, and then taking action. And afterwards, progress continues by returning to see these same people again and again.

Take stock, set your vision, and have a clear message

Often, when getting into a new job, there are several activities that I have found work for me. First of all, I need to walk around and get a feel for the people, the place and the issues. Much of this is reactionary. What I mean is that there is no formal process other than keeping your eyes open, and being sensitive to what you see, what you hear and what you learn. As you do this walk-around, with senses alive for input, things will start to jump out at you.

You will notice housekeeping, facility conditions, orderliness (or the lack of it), and general appearances. You will notice attitudes, body language and commentary. You will notice consistency or inconsistency in the way things are done. You must internally measure all of these observations against some expectation or standard that you maintain. How does this site compare with the best you've seen? How do these people react to seeing you, and to talking with you (comfortable, fearsome, open or closed)?

What does the data show you? Obviously, the assessment of your department, business and its people is not just soft subjective stuff, developing a master plan from the gut, but rather a mix of soft and hard. What does the data for the plant or business say? What has been the track record? What are the weak points that need to be shored-up or dramatically fixed? The combination of field observations, personal discussions, review of the historical data and of the future challenges will allow you to begin a master plan for building on the group's strengths and fixing what is broken. Ultimately, the people will solve the problems. You must connect with them, and that is best done with visibility and a clear message.

In a manufacturing environment, I have found a basic three-pronged message works best. I focus on Safety (personal safety and environmental safety for the community), Cost Control (profit improvement, discipline with spending, frugality) and Quality Control (product quality as well as the quality of personal interactions with customers both internal and external).

My speeches to the troops would often begin with a flip-chart or white-board diagram of a triangle, where each corner had one of these three key priorities, safety, quality and cost. At the center of the triangle was a heart, which symbolized that at the heart (center) of this focus were the people who made up the business unit. They are the core of our company, and the problem-solvers for our future. The message was brief, as you would use for a typical elevator speech (a short commentary that can be completed in a few seconds while the elevator passes through the floors to its destination). Be clear, be concise, be consistent.

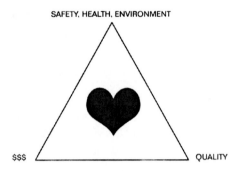

Communicate your vision with a clear and concise message.

A simple diagram, and concise statement of purpose, will help others to capture your vision and understand the necessary action plan. Although a complex message is difficult to grasp, an eye-catching logo or symbol that represents a core message is easy to remember, follow and pursue. Boil it down, formulate your concept and consistently deliver it face-to-face whenever possible.

Know your people

In my walks through the organization, I reiterated this message day by day and person by person. When first put in charge of a manufacturing plant, I always had someone prepare a list of names for me. I wanted to know who was on each shift, who was in each department, and when these employees would be available to be seen. Aside from learning about my new job, I made it a daily priority to walk the plant and meet every person, checking him or her off the master list as I traveled the site.

In the typical 80/20 fashion, within a few days I had seen most of the day shift personnel in each department. But in order to see all 100% within the organization, it was necessary to extend the day into the evening and graveyard shifts as well as getting in to the plant early, stopping in control rooms, shops and other worksites. Whether it was a small plant of 100 people, or later in my career with larger plants of nearly 800 workers, my first priority was to meet each person individually, not just in a big group meeting. I learned more from these tours than years of studying reports ever could have accomplished.

It was common to hear comments from workers such as "This is the first time I have ever had a plant manager come to my area and talk with me," or "I have not seen the prior plant managers in years!" With this face-to-face visibility and connection, there is a unique level of awareness for me and for them. I learn, and they learn. These inputs to me greatly refine and calibrate all the other data that I get from staff, from reports and from customers. Accordingly, better decision-making is possible, leading to better and quicker results.

For their part, the employees get to hear management's message from the horse's mouth, and gain a sense of my passion for my beliefs and value systems such as safety, cost and quality. My message gets life, rather than just one more watered-down and filtered slogan from the head office.

The weather or reality?

I have often told others who wanted to learn about how to manage better, that it is critical to be face-to-face with your people on a regular basis. If you only see them in the workplace occasionally, you can expect one of the following two kinds of conversations. One is shallow, about the weather, sports or other non-critical subjects. If the people don't really have a comfort factor with you, then the discussions are all superficial, similar to small-talk at a party where you do not know the other people and you are all playing nice.

The second kind of conversation you might also expect, if you are seldom accessible to the troops, and if one of the employees has a beef, is an explosion of emotion with all the problems that the person has pent-up inside. This may be his or her one chance to unload on you, so you can hear and solve this person's problem. Accordingly, he or she grabs this rare opportunity (and grabs you) for all that is possible to obtain during this fleeting moment. Neither the small talk nor the explosion is productive.

However, regular, consistent and frequent visits through the organization will have employees feeling more at-home and comfortable with you as a person. As you learn about their families, hobbies, interests, and concerns, your discussions with them about work and about life will take on more meaning. You gain their respect as a person, as you also gain respect for each of them as a person. Comments, opinions and perspectives will have more context and value and thereby can be factored into your overall master plan for continuous improvement.

One word of caution here: always keep the normal structure for chain of command and routine problem-solving channels working as the primary method for issue resolution. Otherwise, you will become the person who solves all problems that are presented every day to you on your walks. It is okay to hear about specifics, and bring them to the attention of the organization. However, just because people surface something to you, this should not distort the overall system for identifying priorities, or rupture the authority of the immediate supervisor who should normally be addressing these issues.

In fact, a good question to ask the employee is "Have you talked to your supervisor about this issue yet?" If so, you may discover problems in the organization's process for problem resolution. If the employee has not yet talked to his or her supervisor about this concern, nor used the company's routine process for initiating work requests, this may be your chance to reinforce the normal way to get things solved. Be sure to give the heads-up to the supervisor, to allow for a more productive response to be generated when the employee brings this issue to the attention of his or her supervisor.

Make it a routine, and your personal priority

It is easy to get trapped in the office. In order to be out in the field, you must find the time that works for you. I often would do my rounds first thing in the morning, catching the graveyard shift before they left work, before I became absorbed in the tasks of the day. Or else I would do the walks right after lunch, before getting tied up for the afternoon. Other times I would make the rounds at the end of the day, seeing the evening shift, which just arrived, and wrap-up my day with productive conversation along the way.

Change your patterns too. Don't walk the same route and at the same time and always from the same direction. See things from different perspectives, making sure that you get to the remote locations that are often neglected. Sit down and chat for a while, rather than just touch-base and march forward. If you want meaningful discussion, you need to stay for a bit. Although this may seem as if it's a big investment of your limited time, it may be the best investment you can make.

What you learn in these visibility visits may save you hours or days of less productive time spent in the office or during meetings. You will be more effective in problem solving with the staff and professionals based on your personal insights and experiences. Most important is that you will see how much quicker you can make a difference in making change happen.

Catch them in the act – of doing things correctly

While you are doing the walk around, do it with a purpose. Aside from the spontaneity of discussing topics that surface during your personal interactions, have a master plan in mind for each walk. It might be a particular theme that you want to pass along, such as the results from last month, and what we must all focus on during the coming month. Or the theme might be a particular area of safety awareness that needs reinforcing. Manage your theme depending on your needs for improvement plant-wide or business-wide.

Where behavior modification is needed, to improve performance, try to catch your people in the act of doing the right behaviors. As discussed in Chapter 6, this is what behavior modification is all about: positively reinforcing behaviors that move closer to the right target. Shape the behavior with your feedback to the employees. Look for the small improvements in the right direction, talk them up, and check these behaviors again on future walks. In time the steady progress will multiply, momentum builds and favorable inertia drives the organization forward to success. This is only possible in the field where the behaviors are going on. You must be present to win. You must be visible to achieve.

A surprise is good once in a while too

Visibility comes in many forms. Aside from routinely being seen around your workplace, visibility also can be an unexpected action you take.

I remember one time we had an important new customer coming to our plant. We knew this was going to be a critical visit, and thought about what we could do to make a positive first impression. Long story short, we decided to have our local elementary school (where we were volunteer sponsors in an Adopt A School program) help us win the hearts and minds of our potential customer.

When the customer arrived at the plant, we had the school's brass band give them a welcome from the front steps of the administration building. You can imagine the surprise and sense of importance experienced by these customers. They probably felt the same as a president does when welcomed to a foreign land and the band plays the national anthem. The faces of the customers beamed. The sales department got the order and we had a new customer.

Of course, the successful outcome was not just from the brass band. We had to be a low-cost, safe, quality provider of their products, but the spirit and visibility we showed them made a favorable impression. They could sense our interest in them, and it was sincere. This is the same as the walking around, with sincerity, interest, and passion about the topics discussed. It does make a difference. You can make a difference.

What works for a plant site also works for a business

Visibility counts in business unit success too. I remember when I was first taking over a failing business unit and had to make rapid changes to survive. Too many of our customers had long-since given up on our ability to produce a quality product that met their needs, and they were gradually shifting more of their business to our competitors. Unless we quickly regained their faith in us, our operations in North America, Europe and Asia would be lost to the competition. How do you regain faith? Face-to-face!

While simultaneously working the inside issues, visiting our manufacturing plants around the globe and meeting with our department heads to learn about problems and solutions, I also began a tour of all key customers. My objective was two-fold: (1) to listen, and (2) to instill confidence in our future.

The face-to-face fact-finding works the same in business as it does in manufacturing. You need to be visible and open to listen to the input from those around you. There is no better way to learn what the customer needs than to ask them. By making the customer rounds, together with my sales and technical experts, I was able to hear the concerns for myself, while my key staff personnel were hearing it at the same time. Later my staff and I could compare notes to build our strategy for corrective action. Sometimes just letting the customers vent, to share their frustrations, is the first step to opening the door to improved relationships.

The second part of face-to-face interaction was to provide my vision first-hand. Each customer was able to see where we intended to go. I was able to explain our new direction that was focused on responsiveness, product development, cost reduction, quality improvement and service. Once again, a clear, concise focused message enabled customers to see how it would improve our utility to them.

One shot is not enough. Just as in the manufacturing environment, where repeat contact and follow-up are necessary, so too is this recipe required for customer relations. We had to deliver. And we did.

Working the issues in-house and making frequent follow-up visits to the customers, we steadily strengthened their sense of confidence in our ability to meet their needs. They knew they were being heard, and they saw the changes. We were able to secure contract continuations, then new contracts, and eventually entirely new business. Our reputation grew, we re-gained market share, and within a year we turned an unprofitable business unit into a profit center with growth and a new future. I am convinced that this visibility at each customer was an important element of our success.

Of course, visibility at home works too

The same as at the plant, or in business, your leadership visibility at home with your children also counts. Are you spending face-to-face time with them as they enjoy their hobbies, or as they struggle with their homework? Do you set aside quality time to hear their concerns and provide guidance on how problems can be resolved in constructive ways? Is your family vision, mission and plan well understood regarding values, priorities and the reality of limited resources? Does the family team understand your expectations, and benefit from your positive reinforcement as you see each member doing his or her share of contribution to this master plan? Are you shaping behaviors as you do your walks around the house? Your instructive visibility can make change happen at home as well as at the plant, office or headquarters.

Leadership visibility counts too

Be eager to accept leadership roles. It is a smart way to make a difference with issues about which you feel strongly. Leverage your leadership; pull the rope (pull the team forward). Your leadership enables faster results than "pushing on a rope." The more you are hidden within an organization structure the more difficult it is to influence the organization's overall direction. By stepping out in front, taking charge of issues and situations, you have the strength to make change happen. Pull a group forward with your strength of purpose and direction. Take charge. Get your input, show your vision, and lead.

Like the tree in the forest, for the sound to be heard without doubt, someone must be there. In a work environment, to make change happen, you must be seen by your team, by your peers, by your customers and supervisors. The more visible you are in your own department, reinforcing your vision for the future, clarifying your goals and aspirations for the team, and providing your feedback when your performers are on track or derailed, then your likelihood of success will soar. Likewise, the more visible you are to your external customers, the more they will be confident of what you and your company represent to their own success.

Your ability to get out and be seen will make all the difference in your speed of implementing change at work and at home. At times, your visibility across the office threshold of your supervisor or with others of authority will make a difference too, so don't be afraid to be seen in these environments as well. The boss won't bite. This is the topic for discussion in the next chapter, "Cross The Threshold."

Chapter 11
Cross the Threshold

The boss won't bite

As George Addair said, *"Everything you've ever wanted is on the other side of fear."*

In other words, you have to cross that barrier of fear to achieve the dreams of your life, time and time again. You would like to go on a date with what appears to be your first love, but you fear rejection. You want to advance your education, but fear leaving home to attend a far-away university. You want to change your job, but worry about the uncertainties. Aspirations can be achieved, but that step of facing the fear and crossing to the other side will separate those who succeed from those who just dream.

For many employees, crossing the office threshold of their supervisor raises the anxiety level, so they avoid this authority figure as often as possible. Some people avoid the boss at all costs. Why stick your neck out needlessly?

But the truth is, it is important to maintain a close relationship with your boss in order to better understand the supervisor's vision, needs and expectations. Ideally, when you can anticipate your supervisor's needs and take initiative, you will then be well on your way to being perceived as a key contributor. Let's consider the issue of office geography, the degree that you encourage your team to access you, as well as the importance of being close to your own boss.

Geography, near, far and near

Early in your career, it is likely that you will be near your boss, with offices in the same building. Later in your career, the boss may be located at the main office or at company headquarters, remote from your own department. Further along in your career, you too may be at the corporate headquarters, so that the top person or your boss are once again nearby. Given the choice, try to locate as close as possible to your supervisor. Ideally, your boss will be in the next office down the hall. This gives you easy access to be part of informal hallway conversations, spur-of-the-moment brainstorming, and similar random opportunities of exposure that generate closeness and synergy of thought and action.

By the same token, your own team may be near or far. You need to be near your team for the same reasons: you want to have access to the pulse of what is going on in your group, you want to know issues as they are surfacing, and you want to be accessible to your team so you and they can readily kick around ideas as problems or opportunities surface.

If torn between whether to locate next to your boss, or next to your staff, the answer is that "It depends." It depends on many factors, including the state of your staff with relation to your vision, values and plans. If the members of your staff are new to you, and you sense that there will be a lot of work to get them to do things and see things with your set of priorities and strategies, then stay close to them. You can find other ways to stay close to your boss.

However, if the staff seems to be working well as a unit with common and consistent values, consistent with your own approach to the future, then there is less need for you to be routinely there to monitor and influence daily decision making. You can locate closer to the supervisor (to get closer to this level's values and plans) and stay in touch with your own staff as needed.

Sounding board

There is benefit to supervisor and subordinate having an open relationship where each can use the other as a sounding board. It is not a one-way street.

As you are considering taking steps to make changes, it helps to know that your plans will not be blocked from above. With proximity to your boss, and a casual open relationship of free communications, you will be able to get early signals. If your master plan could potentially be sidetracked, due to obstacles that you might learn about from conversations with the boss, then you can adjust your strategy accordingly. Test the waters early to get feedback and direction. Don't be afraid to cross that threshold. Benefit from the supervisor's input. We covered the value of this progressive approach in Chapter 1, "Slice the Salami."

Cross the threshold. All you want may be there.

Similarly, when you have plans that can impact the organization below you, use one or more of your trusted team members to help you generate ideas and sense reactions to how your plans may roll out. Over time, you will learn to seek, find and trust the honest and candid feedback of key staff members. You will discover which ones have the courage to tell you if they think your idea stinks, or whether it simply has some flaws that need addressing before implementation. Reach out to these individuals. They are your true friends and helpers. Those who always tell you that your ideas are perfect will be the ones who get you into trouble. In addition, be careful how you react to a subordinate's feedback. Listen and thoughtfully evaluate what he or she says, so that this person will feel comfortable being open with you, and will continue to do so.

The atmosphere you set, particularly when subordinates cross your office threshold, will determine the frequency with which you gain access to their input and perspectives. You want that clear view to their thoughts and opinions, in order to cultivate the right atmosphere. Help demolish barriers to entry. Your expanding pool of data and input will help you make better decisions.

Just as you will gravitate to the people whose feedback and input you trust, so too will your supervisor. Work to become the one your supervisor can trust for open, honest, helpful feedback. Don't be afraid to give candid input to your boss. Let the two-way street of crossing office thresholds accelerate the level of trust and communication between you and your subordinates, and between you and your boss. Pass to the other side of fear, and encourage your subordinates to do the same, by reinforcing them when they do so, and all will benefit from the ability to find more success.

If you have a boss who does not appreciate candid feedback, and you get signals of discontent when you offer input, then it may be necessary to modify your approach. Constructively work the relationship to find the most effective way to keep communication channels open between you and your boss, and you and your own work-team.

In the spirit of visibility, as discussed in the prior chapter, when you do your walking around, be sure to stop in to various offices, sit down, and chat. This routine of crossing the threshold and letting people talk with you, as you listen to their points of view, will further strengthen the depth of input and perspective you obtain (and increases your chance to reinforce your objectives and visions). At the same time, your presence and familiarity will decrease the fear factor in these individuals, and they too will be less hesitant to cross your office threshold to chat with you. Greater access and greater openness all enhance the database for better decision-making.

Being comfortable with crossing the threshold and talking with your boss is one thing, but how you follow-through on what you say, once you are there, may well be the most important skill you must develop. We'll discuss this in the next chapter, "Don't Forget!"

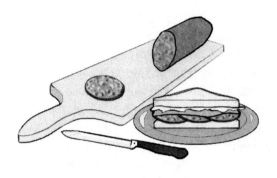

Chapter 12
Don't Forget!

My word is my bond

The topic focus in this chapter may well be the most important in this book for your career development and your personal life, and thus a critical skill to master. It's all about commitment. The ability to remember a commitment made, and to follow-through on that obligation, separates the leaders from the losers.

In our professional and personal lives it is not about what we say (we will do), but what we actually do. At work, this is easily measured in the annual performance reviews, which evaluate goals (commitments) and accomplishments (results). More informally, your routine behaviors establish expectations from others, based on what you typically do, which becomes a measure of your performance as well. When you say "I'll have it for you by next Friday," your track record either gets a positive or negative rating when Friday comes, depending upon whether you have met or missed your commitment.

In personal relationships, it is the same. You can probably identify right now a handful of friends or relatives who you know can fit into one of two categories: those who consistently do, and those who promise but more often do not do.

Of course, both in and out of work it is seldom black and white. There are ranges of performance in all of us. However, to excel in your profession and in your interpersonal relationships, the more you are seen as a person whose word is golden, the more you will be the person who is respected, appreciated and promoted.

Process and Priority

During my seminars on this topic I have often had fun with my audience and asked a question such as this: "Please raise your hand if you are confident that you have a functional follow-up system that will assure that you can send me an email to say "I did it!" 4 years from now, on this date, at 2:45 in the afternoon local time." As you can imagine, most of the hands stay down. We addressed this issue a bit in Chapter 3, relating to time management.

Although these seminars were back before high-tech aids such as Blackberries, iPhones, and other newer electronic devices that can be set to give you a reminder on a specific date and time, the point of my question is still valid today. Whether or not you utilize reminders that are high-tech or low-tech (accordion files, Post-it® notes, or a scribbled message on your calendar), you must have a process to capture commitments and have them surface when you need the reminder. **This is your first step. Get a system.** This is the *process* part of the equation. You need a fail-safe process that will store your obligations and prompt you to action in time to meet the need.

Do you have a fail-safe process? Do you give it priority?

The other part of the equation is the *priority* portion. You may have that reminder pop up and tell you to do something, but **it takes your personal action to set the priority to do the task.** If either the process or the priority breaks down, then the commitment is not met, and your performance reflects poorly compared with the original expectation.

"I will try to....?" No! "I will!"

In fact, let's talk a bit about how that commitment is made in the first place. As was mentioned in Chapter 4, about attitude, one common failure is to use the expression "I will try to (do something)...." This is basically a non-commitment. Get in the habit of making commitments, not making weak excuses for yourself even before you get started. Rather than say "I'll try to call you this afternoon," establish the habit to modify your speech patterns and say, "I'll call you this afternoon." Then set your reminder system in place (the process) and do it (give it a priority).

Verbal contracts

When you commit by saying that you will do something for someone else, you have made a verbal contract. How you then perform is either consistent with the contract, thereby providing customer satisfaction, or it is a breach of contract, resulting in customer dissatisfaction. The customer may be your supervisor, your subordinate, your peer, your friend or a family member. Once you say you will do something, the other party has an expectation. Then, either you do it or you don't. It is all about your word and your actions.

When working with new staff members, I typically have a clarifying conversation with each person about my own expectations for commitments and our verbal contracts. My commentary follows this path:

"Unless I have a hard deadline with short time-frame, I will usually first ask you when you can have a task completed rather than say you must get this task done by X date." Note, it is always best to have the other person tell you when he or she thinks it is possible to have a task done, rather than to ask if he or she can have something done by X date. Why? Because, particularly when you are the boss, once you ask a subordinate if he or she can do it by your requested date you run the risk that the individual will want to please the boss, and agree to your date with the hope that he or she can meet the target. It is your date the person is striving for, in place of a date to which this individual has committed.

There is one other point about the other person specifying the date. At times the task is quite complex, and it is not easy for someone to just reply on-the-spot with a date. In these cases, your request to the person should be in two parts: (1) give me a date, when you will give me a date, and (2) at that date, give me the target date for the completion of the project. For example, the individual can tell you that it will take a week for him or her to scope out the task, and in a week will give you the completion target for this project.

In either case, after setting the stage by asking my team members for the date of completion of a project, I then continue with my explanation and expectations as follows,

"When you say you will have the task to me by a certain date, I will not normally bother you again, and will expect to see the project completed how and when you said you would. As long as we have this understanding, all is fine. The problem begins when you are late, so let's address this now, up-front, to assure we can avoid any unnecessary misunderstanding.

"Remember, the date you give me may either be just for my own use, or it may be a date that I in-turn commit to others, since your project may be part of a larger activity where others are making their plans and commitments based on our contribution to the overall objective. Accordingly, the date you give me may not only impact me and my plans, but those of others as well, and any downstream commitments they make to others.

"I understand that uncertainties in the project or other competing demands may start to put you behind in your project timing. That is part of the real world. However, you have an obligation to me to alert me well in advance of the deadline. Be prepared to tell me what the new potential date might be. This does not mean that you will be granted the extension requested, so be sure that you surface the problem early enough so that you leave yourself a cushion to make adjustments to still meet the original date.

"When you ask for an extension to the deadline, I will then have two possible responses. One will be to grant you the additional time. Lucky you! However, the other response may be that due to commitments

that I have made, or constraints that you are not aware of, the date is critical and it can not change. My role may be to grant you relief on your other conflicting priorities, to let these other projects wait until you complete the issue in question, or to grant you more resources. Accordingly, please come prepared to give me an overview of why you cannot make the deadline, with your own suggestions of what is needed in order to meet the committed date. Together we will resolve the conflicts.

"Please do not ever put me in a position to learn about the late completion at a time when it is no longer possible to juggle priorities or add resources and still make the deadline. I respect timely discussions to allow flexibility either to extend the date or to modify overall priorities. I do not respect the surprise of a missed target date with no room to solve the problem."

This up-front understanding has generally been sufficient to keep things running smoothly, to eliminate surprises and avoid frustration. Most activities are not so critical that a late project will create great problems. However, frequent late projects always reflect poorly on the person who has failed to accomplish the task as committed. So, the rules for you should be:

1. Set a reasonable date, considering all your other obligations (remember the guidance in Chapter 4 to be pessimistic when dealing with time estimates).

2. Monitor your progress throughout the task to assure on-time completion is likely (use your process of follow-up and time-management, as discussed in Chapter 3, to check if you have completed key stages of the task consistent with your original estimates).

3. As soon as potential delays are evident, begin a conversation with the other person to whom you have made the verbal contract.

4. Either negotiate a new date, or have the other person help you with readjusting priorities and resources so that the original date can be met.

With your consistent application of your own personal system of follow-up, and with your dedication to prioritizing verbal commitments to others, you will establish a consistent history showing that you are someone whose word is your bond. This will gain you respect, credibility and honor among co-workers, family and friends. This may be the most important skill you can refine. Do it! (In other words, don't *try* to do it!).

As you work your follow-up systems, and meet deadlines, you will find that your management of time improves too. Ideally, you will be able to carve out more discretionary time, which can also be applied to career development, life-work balance or other self-defined priorities. This is the topic of the next chapter.

Chapter 13
Discretionary Time

It's all about you

So often in our busy work environment and personal life, we are focused on meeting obligations to others. Whether it be the daily, weekly or monthly report, or preparing the annual budget, or getting the kids to their after-school activities, we don't seem to have time for ourselves. Then we wonder, "Why do I feel so stressed and tired?" We visualize ourselves as guinea pigs running in treadmills and getting nowhere fast.

Discretionary time, however, is all about you. It is about carving out some special time to relax, at your own discretion, to think, reboot your internal hard-drive, or do whatever works for you to re-charge the batteries. This is critical to productive and creative thinking and problem solving. Ever wonder why you go to bed at night with an unsolved problem, and wake up the next morning with the answer? It can be the same during waking hours: take a break, let the subconscious work in the background, and let the solution pop to the surface. Additionally, let the body heal itself with a relaxing break.

Discretionary time is time you set aside to do things *you* want to do, with a focus on *planning*, rather than on *doing*. This is distinguished from time you spend on imposed tasks, cranking out the routine mandates of your job or your tasks at home. I am not talking here about setting time during your day to follow your to-do list, working on yet another backlog of things you have to do for others to meet your objectives and goals.

Instead, I am talking about time you set aside for yourself, to think about your overall priorities, your plan for the coming day or week. Maybe it is a subtle distinction, but this is important: *planning* for the coming week or for tomorrow, is different from *doing* a to-do activity. Even though the plan may mostly be related to tasks for others, the step of planning is for yourself, that act of organizing priorities, evaluating what to do first, last, or not at all, and providing order to your coming activities. It's as if you are defragging your body's hard drive, to get things organized and more efficient.

How do you begin getting time for discretionary time?

It may seem at first as if it is a "Catch-22," where you need time to have time to get time. It's true! At first, if all you are doing is fighting fires, you will never break out of that spiral. You have to take control and initiate the change. Do it a slice at a time. Slice the salami with a small but manageable bite of time you set aside for yourself.

You may find on Friday afternoons, when the rest of the world may be trying to wrap-up their week, and they too may be self-focused on cleaning things up before the weekend, that your typical interruptions decrease somewhat. Take advantage of this momentary lull, close your office door, and give yourself fifteen minutes of quiet alone-time to plan.

Look at what you have accomplished this week, compared with your overall goals, and look ahead to next week. What needs to be carried over, to get done when you return to the office? What new things pop up in your follow-up system for the coming days, and how will you prioritize these within the many things you hope to accomplish? Plan a bit also for your personal life. Use this quiet quarter hour to consider as well your family, friends and personal activities with which you want to progress. Let this be the time to order those tickets to the play you have wanted to see or to make a dinner reservation at your favorite restaurant. This is your fifteen minutes of freedom. Enjoy it.

Another technique is to simply take a walk during lunch. Get out from behind the desk, get out to fresh air or at least a change of scenery, and walk for ten minutes. You'll find you can do a lot of productive thinking when you are alone, walking, without other distractions. Perhaps avoid the elevator, and take the stairs. Exercise for the body, recuperation for the mind. Smell the roses!

Eventually, you will have added short routines to your day and week that allow you to capture your own discretionary time. The sensation will be noticeable. Make the disconnect and the rest will follow.

It's a question of priorities

Be sure to give yourself a priority for your private time, and for other important priorities in your life. Do not just let the outside world, the pull of the job, or the pressures at home, be the only force that moves you. Take control. Do things for yourself. You set these priorities, so be sure to have them right.

Here is an item I have seen passed along by friends through the Internet (author unknown), relating to setting life priorities. I hope this message sticks with you:

"TWO GLASSES OF WINE

When things in your life seem almost too much to handle, when 24 hours in a day are not enough, remember the mayonnaise jar and the 2 glasses of wine...

A professor stood before his philosophy class and had some items in front of him. When the class began, he wordlessly picked up a very large and empty mayonnaise jar and proceeded to fill it with golf balls.

He then asked the students if the jar was full. They agreed that it was.

The professor then picked up a box of pebbles and poured them into the jar. He shook the jar lightly. The pebbles rolled into the open areas between the golf balls. He then asked the students again if the jar was full. They agreed it was.

The professor next picked up a box of sand and poured it into the jar. Of course, the sand filled up everything else He asked once more if the jar was full. The students responded with a unanimous "yes."

The professor then produced two glasses of wine from under the table and poured the entire contents into the jar, effectively filling the empty space between the sand. The students laughed.

"Now," said the professor, as the laughter subsided, "I want you to recognize that this jar represents your life. The golf balls are the important things; your family, your children, your health, your friends, and your favorite passions; things that if everything else was lost and only they remained, your life would still be full.

The pebbles are the other things that matter like your job, your house, and your car. The sand is everything else; the small stuff.

"If you put the sand into the jar first," he continued, *"There is no room for the pebbles or the golf balls. The same goes for life. If you spend all your time and energy on the small stuff, you will never have room for the things that are important to you. Pay attention to the things that are critical to your happiness. Play with your children. Take time to get medical checkups. Take your partner out to dinner. Play another 18. Do one more run down the ski slope. There will always be time to clean the house and fix the disposal. Take care of the golf balls first; the things that really matter. Set your priorities. The rest is just sand."*

One of the students raised her hand and inquired what the wine represented.

The professor smiled. "I'm glad you asked. It just goes to show you that no matter how full your life may seem, there's always room for a couple of glasses of wine with a friend."

Share this with a friend."

Have you set your priorities for what really matters?

You are the one filling the mayonnaise jar, or filling your day with activities. Do your activities contribute to your work-life balance and the right priorities?

If not, you need to do something about this, and make a change. It can begin with the fifteen minutes a week of quiet discretionary time, if nothing more than to start the planning process. Then one slice at a time you can add more discretionary time to your routines, and implement important life-changes that make a difference.

Keep a diary of successes

Before ending this theme of discretionary time, let me suggest that one of the things you can do every day, or at least once a week during your time-out, is to jot down some of your successes. Your documentation may be that you finally took the time for your own discretionary time in the office, or it may be that you crossed the threshold of your boss to talk about a future project, or it may be any one of a number of items that made you feel proud or happy.

Why bother to keep this log? Two reasons:

(1) The success sheet can serve as a handy reference when it comes time to prepare your performance review goal status update, assuming that your corporation requires status updates. Even if your company does not have a formal program, having such a summary is still a good practice to follow. Although our corporate process really only required one time per year to formalize the documentation of results versus goals, I had a habit of volunteering updates to my bosses through the years once every quarter. I asked my staff as well to prepare their goal updates to me on a quarterly basis. This keeps all of us formally looking at our annual targets at least quarterly, allowing us to make necessary course corrections and persistently pursue progress. The daily or weekly success sheet served as a nice way to jot down progress when it was happening, and to refer to it when it was necessary to prepare the quarterly and annual performance reports.

(2) The second reason to keep notes of your successes is that it provides you with some personal positive reinforcement and inspiration. This works fine for the at-home person as well, where corporate goal documentation is not required (unless you have a unique spousal relationship at home!). Often, with so many things that can go wrong and so many challenges occupying our minds, we easily lose sight of the headway we are making. We focus on the negative, get down on ourselves, and feel more stressed. Take a breath! Sit back and reflect on the small successes that build up to bigger ones. Make yourself look for your movement in the right direction, to shape your own behavior with positive reinforcement. Be your own mentor, coach and motivator. The list helps.

Your use of discretionary time allows you to refine your skills with renewed focus. You can pin-point the areas where you want to prioritize your efforts and actions. This can be a focus in fundamental leadership basics, such as knowing your people and your job details well. Your discretionary time can also be to dream about new initiatives to undertake. Alternatively, this time can also be spent laying out your personal plans to make small or big changes that can generate important improvements for you and your team, or for you and your family or friends.

There are dozens of focus areas where you can apply the best use of your private think-time. Our next chapter, The Three Eyes (I's), will address these integrated layers of leadership skills, and with the aid of an easy to remember symbol, you can think through what you want to consider during your discretionary time.

Chapter 14
The Three Eyes (I's)

A leadership symbol to remember, and practice

The accompanying graphic depicts a man with three eyes, and a triangle divided into three sections, with lines at the bottom, an eye in the middle of the triangle, and an upward pointing arrow at the top. This diagram is intended to provide you with an image that you can recall, which will simultaneously trigger the key points of this chapter. The three-eyed man is simply to remember the three letters, "I," each standing for one of three concepts from this pyramid of leadership skills.

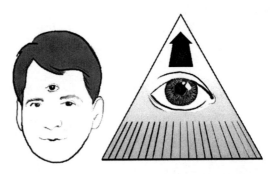

Leadership: Involvement, imagination and initiative

What do each of the layers of the triangle and symbols represent in relation to effective leadership on or off the job?

Involvement

- Foundation layer (many lines, similar to columns, at the base of the pyramid): Involvement.

- The lines represent the many fundamentals, or pillars, that are important to a strong leadership foundation, such as:

  o Know the details of your job or role well.

  o Know the people with whom you interact.

  o Understand the competencies for success in your formal job and in your leadership roles away from the office.

  o Be excellent in the basics of your job or tasks, and execute the necessary responsibilities with attention to detail and customer satisfaction.

  o Achieve your goals and objectives, consistent with SMART (and not DUMB) goals:

    ▪ S = Specific

    ▪ M = Measured (quantifiable)

    ▪ A = Achievable (reasonable)

    ▪ R = Relevant (consistent with company goals)

    ▪ T = Timed (able to be done when needed)

  o And not DUMB goals:

    ▪ D = Disengaged (not consistent with the needs of the company)

    ▪ U = Unfocused (impossible to measure)

    ▪ M = Monumental (too big to achieve in a lifetime)

- B = Beyond control (neither the individual nor the company have the resources to achieve the goal)
  o Or another way DUMB goals have been defined:
    - **D**angerously **U**nattainable, **M**onstrously **B**ig goals
  o A good goal must have all five constructive characteristics to be a SMART goal, but need only have one of these poor characteristics to be DUMB.
  o *Caution:* expertise only in this foundation layer of the pyramid is not enough to be a good leader. Experts who stay at this level are simply good bureaucrats. They know the details, they know the rules, but perhaps nothing more.

Imagination

- Middle layer (the eye): Imagination.
  o The eye signifies *vision.*
  o Look to the future and dream about what can be done to provide improvements in the work environment and at home and in the community.
    - As you look around your workplace, organization, household and community do a mental gap analysis.
    - Then use your imagination to figure out how you can close the gap with programs, plans and the training and development of your team (employees, family, friends).
  o See how to make change happen for continuous improvement.

o Visualize your continuous learning opportunities, so that you can continue to grow in your skills and capabilities for the future.

o Visualize how you and your group can or should be, relative to your internal standard, and how long it should take you to get to this new level.

o *Caution*: though important to organizational and personal growth, expertise in this middle layer of the pyramid is not enough. If you stop at this layer, although you are better than a bureaucrat is, you are still trapped in dreams. Dreams are not results. An effective leader makes things happen! You must move to the top level.

Initiative

• Top of the pyramid (depicted by the upward pointing arrow): Initiative.

o The arrow signifies *action!*

o This is the symbol of the true leader:

▪ Knows his or her function and role well, built on a strong foundation.

▪ Understands the details of the job, tasks and key success factors.

▪ Dreams about the future and has a clear vision of how to make improvements, *and*

▪ Takes action:

• Makes things happen.

• Works on continuous improvement.

• Seeks new methods and techniques for success.

- Sets goals and works towards their achievement.

- Implements change!

A well grounded and effective leader

The effective leader in the office, at home and in the community is well grounded in the leadership pyramid of "The Three Eyes" (Involvement, Imagination, Initiative). He or she has solid foundations, good vision for the future and takes action. These basics are combined with a strong service orientation (the four-to-one rule) to internal and external customers, peers, subordinates and supervisors, family and friends. In addition, strong leaders have learned to manage their time well, including carving out some alone-time for themselves, as discretionary time, to plan for the next day and for their future with work-life balance in mind.

These leaders have learned that to make change happen, a bit at a time (slice the salami), coupled with positive reinforcement, they can make a great difference in overall effectiveness, for themselves and for those around them. Also, when a sense of urgency is demanded, effective leaders know how to light the fire under their team with passionate, sincere and clear communications that are targeted to the motivations of each person in their group, and they anticipate what might be potential filters to good communications, and use communication strategies that surpass these obstacles. They also know the value of the strength of a team working together. They make the effort to engage all the members of their team as appropriate to obtain optimal solutions to tricky problems, and to capitalize on developing opportunities.

Confident leaders are unafraid to cross the threshold of their boss, passing through to the other side of whatever fears they may face, and visit with others who can help them, as they brainstorm ideas or simply seek mentors to help guide their own future. Such leaders keep a positive can-do attitude as they face difficulties, and they let themselves be visible and available to their employees, encouraging open discussion beyond shallow comments about the weather or just venting about the problem of the day. These leaders strive for continuous improvement within their function, of their team and of themselves, in part from continuous learning. They are dedicated to a consistent system of follow-up and action, with a track record of meeting obligations, such that their word is their bond.

These outstanding leaders thereby become the supervisor everyone wants to work for, the peer everyone wants to help and receive support from, and the subordinate every boss wants on his or her team. People with the attributes of the three I's also become the friend or family member that all seek out for comfort, support and companionship. By exercising each of the dozen or more principles outlined in this book so far, you too will continue to refine your leadership and interpersonal skills for long-term success at work, and for contentment in your personal life.

"Slice the Salami – tips for life and leadership, one slice at a time," offered the specifics of each of these concepts within the previous chapters. What follows now is a more detailed guide to help you prepare to take an interview, or if you are an interviewer, how to give an interview (Chapter 15 - Part I, and Chapter 16 - Part II), as well as show you how to improve your résumé, in Chapter 17. The book then wraps-up with a chapter on ethics and values, and closes with encouragement to enjoy your life and be happy.

Please read on and slice a few more pieces of knowledge to whet your appetite for wisdom and skills for success.

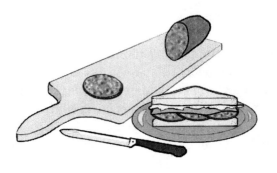

Chapter 15

How to Prepare for an Interview – Part I

Three Key Concepts

Time to work

This chapter and the next will be different from the other chapters. You will have to work! In the prior chapters, you may have been reading in a more casual way, considering which specific techniques to try once you set the book down. As we have already discussed, active learning sticks with you much longer, so I do hope that you have been trying new things at work and off the job too as you discovered tips from this book. These next two chapters, however, are different. I ask you to do some exercises *while* you are working your way through the chapters.

You will get the most out of these next two important chapters by being more engaged in the details, doing some fun exercises, and seeking a deep understanding about what you need to do in order to prepare well for a job interview. Go find a pencil and paper, sit up straight, and get ready to be better prepared than all your competitors to capture that next great promotion or job change that you want! If you are now at-home, and are thinking of entering or re-entering a paying career, this is your guidebook to success. What should you do differently with these chapters? If I present a hypothetical question to you, please don't just read on, but actually *stop*, think about the question, and formulate your own answer(s). Then proceed, to see how your perspective agrees with, or is different from, what I am mentioning. If there is a task to do, such as to make a list, do it. Don't just continue reading, but take your pencil and paper and actually create your list. Then read on. You get the idea. Invest in your future by investing now in the details.

Why do more than just read about interviewing techniques? Don't forget the story about my first mentor, Paul Yoon, who shared the saying (see Chapter 7) *"Learn easy, forget easy. Learn hard, remember always."* Likewise, heed the lesson from Chapter 2 about the "Cone of Learning" study, and the importance of active involvement to reinforce retention.

This is not to say that the learning-hard method has to be overbearing, or even over-boring. I encourage you to sink your teeth into these next two chapters so that you can obtain the most out of them. They can really change your life. I know this material has changed the lives of many who have benefited from doing these simple exercises and preparations.

We will cover techniques to help you to be best prepared to take a job interview, if applying for a job vacancy, or to conduct an interview, if you are the hiring manager or anyone in the chain of decision makers selecting the best candidate for a vacancy. First, we will discuss three key concepts. Next, we will review the various parts of a typical interview, and how you can prepare for each specific part. Finally, we will cover how to improve your résumé, but that chapter will not be as intense, and you can relax again (until you actually get into the task of really writing your own résumé!).

Bonus: it's not just about job interviews!

Before getting started in the details, let me point out that the techniques you are about to learn here will apply to more than just job interviews. The pre-interview preparation process, exercises and a form you will use, as well as knowing what to do during each phase of an interview, will also apply to interviews for college or advanced institutions such as business, law and medical schools. Likewise, the specifics of how to improve your résumé also are relevant for the application essays and forms that a prospective student must submit.

I've coached many such pre-entrant individuals to success with these same skills. So if you or someone you know fits this category, then simply substitute "entrance interview" (for college) when you see the words "job interview," and think "entrance application" when you read résumé.

The last few years while working in Chile, I used to volunteer as a guest speaker for a pre-MBA training program that lasted several months for young professionals interested in obtaining an MBA at institutions of higher learning around the world. Graduates of this program typically were awarded entrance to universities in Europe, the United States and Australia.

The businessman who ran this program asked me to be the anchor speaker to prepare the students for the critical activities of submitting an effective application and then handling themselves well during the selection interviews. The same techniques that you are about to learn for job interviews work as well for any sort of screening process where you must competitively demonstrate qualifications and skills.

The positive feedback I received from these participants confirmed that this process works! They were accepted where they wanted to go, and with more comfort and control than they had previously felt during such high-stress and high-stakes challenges. I have gotten the same feedback from job seekers. What you are about to study will make a significant difference in how you prepare and how you perform. These techniques will work for you.

It's not rocket science

The material is not rocket science. In fact, after going through these two chapters, you may reflect over the material and say to yourself, "Gee, there were not many new items that I did not know." However, I hope you will also say, "Wow, with just these few key concepts I have completely changed how I will prepare myself for my next interview!"

In fact, I had the same reaction, changing my approach completely, when I first learned some of these details years ago, and have since refined items further into a basic package of information that works. Let me share a few real-life stories.

I've been advocating these preparation tips for years, and my friends and staff know that I enjoy mentoring and sharing such techniques. One day my secretary told me that the son of her doctor had been trying unsuccessfully for over a year to get a job. The young man had a good résumé, he had the opportunity to interview, but in every case, he failed to get a job offer. She asked if I would mind spending a bit of time with him to coach him to success. I said "Of course. I'd be glad to help!"

I met the doctor's son. We went through my two-hour "How to Prepare for an Interview" review (the same material that you will read in these two chapters). One week later, he had an interview and got the job!

At another time, I had a professional accounting person filling in for a department head who was on maternity leave. The temporary person was helping us, while she got herself ready to apply for full-time jobs elsewhere (we had no job vacancies, or we would have hired her). She was good at her work, but always felt insecure when she went to interviews. She asked me if I could help her get ready for the full-time job interviews. I said "Of course. I'd be glad to help!" I did my workshop with her and soon after, she got her job. I asked her how it went and she told me "Artie, this was the most comfortable I have *ever* felt in taking a job interview. I knew what to expect, I felt ready and in control, and my confidence showed during the whole interview process."

Neither of the two examples I highlighted above were unique. I have enjoyed the same feedback from many others who have learned that knowing what to prepare, and how to communicate your message can make all the difference in the world. In addition, what is particularly important to remember is that the people's life history and job experience did not change during our two-hour training session. What changed was how they handled their preparation, and how they handled the interview itself, with effective, memorable and targeted messages to the interviewer. You can do the same if you do the work in these two chapters.

Note: these basic concepts apply to both an interviewer getting ready to screen candidates for a job, and a job applicant, trying to put a best foot forward during the interview process. I will generally focus on the job applicant side of the equation, which may be more relevant to you and your personal career growth, but you can easily utilize these same concepts to improve your interview selection process if you are the boss looking to hire the best candidate. Let's get started with the first of the three key concepts for interview preparation.

First key concept: Every job has critical skills for success

This seems simple enough. However, I want to take this important concept a piece at a time with you, to be sure it is crystal clear. All else which follows, is based on completely understanding this first concept.

Every job: *every job* has critical skills for success. This means all of them. It doesn't matter whether it is the chief executive officer (CEO) or the janitor, every job has critical skills for success.

What might some of these skills be? Let's do a quick exercise. List several specific skills for a CEO and for a janitor, and then check the list below (Remember: do the work now, don't just read on. Make your list!).

Stop! Think.

What follows are some possible skills that might be critical to success in each of these two jobs.

CEO: strategic planning, business acumen, decision making under stress, negotiating major deals, ethical business practices, strong value systems, skill development of subordinates for succession planning and strength of the organization, budgeting, cross-functional department coordination and integration, public speaking, etc..

Janitor: attention to details, ability to follow specific lists of tasks, adherence to safety and hygiene rules, sufficient mechanical aptitude to handle equipment requirements of the job, consistency in work practices (attendance, on time on the job, etc.)

CEO and janitor each have specific skills for success.

How did you do? Did you have any of the skills listed above? Don't worry if you did not, since this was just a warm-up exercise! Let's keep moving with our clarification of this important definition and concept.

Critical skills: every job has *critical skills* for success. There are some skills, among the many that constitute a job description and overall responsibilities, that are more critical than the rest. These are the skills that can make-or-break a career if done exceptionally well, poorly or not at all.

Any job may have hundreds of skills associated with doing the necessary tasks. Some of these skills may be technical. You may need a particular degree, or experience doing the specialized work, such as a doctor, engineer or teacher. Some skills may relate to the work environment. For example the ability to tolerate long hours of focus under stressful conditions, such as while performing delicate surgery, or completing an emergency repair job. Another work environment issue might be whether the person must interact with many others to get the job done, or whether the person is an individual contributor who primarily works alone. Finally, a third category of skill associated with the environment of the job is travel: whether there is a lot or none.

Let me explain this travel issue for a bit, just to clarify the understanding of skill associated with environmental factors. For decades, I worked in a manufacturing environment, where the chemical plants operated 24 hours per day, 7 days a week, all year long (except for occasional planned downtime for preventive maintenance and system cleanout, or unplanned emergency breakdowns).

As a department head and later plant manager, my duties included 24-hour responsibility. That means that when there was an emergency, there would be times when the job responsibility required me to be onsite. Somehow (I guess we can blame Murphy's Law), the worst problems always seemed to happen at 3 in the morning! I remember many cold and dark nights in Syracuse, New York, when in the middle of a blizzard I would be called out to the plant in the wee hours of the morning due to snow blowing into a high voltage substation, causing a power outage.

Sometimes the work would continue right into the morning, and it became a weary and long day. Other times the problem would be fixed, and there was a chance to return home to catch a few hours of sleep before heading back to work. Of course, additional *skills* associated with this work environment are the ability to function well during sudden emergency conditions, make critical decisions and to remain focused while fatigue sets in. I remember once looking at melting snow, dripping water onto a live and exposed 440-volt copper conductor that was the main source of energy supply to an entire manufacturing unit.

Although this was the middle of the night, on an emergency call-in, I had to sustain laser focus while directing a crew of electricians to shut down the process unit rapidly and safely. However, despite this environment, I nearly always got to return home to my own bed at night. As a manufacturing front-line person, or even plant manager, the job is local.

Later in my career, when I was a vice president and general manager of a plastics molding compound division, I was located at the corporate headquarters. However, my work environment changed drastically from my manufacturing days. Aside from the expected change of being in the corporate offices, always visible to executive managers, and the associated skill-sets needed to survive there, one of my biggest adjustments was travel. All my customers were spread out across the United States and the world.

It was common to begin with a flight out of town at the start of the week, and return home no sooner than Friday night, in order to coordinate a productive series of customer visits. For our overseas customers, the time away from home was even longer. For example, during my first year in this new job, I traveled to Japan four times (as I became involved in negotiating a new joint venture), and these travels typically would last up to two weeks at a time, to maximize the productivity of the visit.

I quickly learned that a new skill associated with success in this job was the ability for me to adjust to travel and time away from home. Fortunately, I have a supportive wife, and together we made the necessary sacrifices and adjustments to survive this particular environmental factor associated with my job. The stress from this extreme change in life style can be a career breaker. Do not underestimate the importance of environmental factors of the job when considering important skills for success.

When my wife and I moved to South America, where I was a general manager for our corporation's business there, we arrived with no Spanish skills, to a completely different culture, and were thousands of miles away from family and friends. Here is another example of a skill that can make or break a person, that is, the ability to adjust to different cultures, as well as the ability to adjust to being far from family. There are similar adjustments needed for success: to survive in a rural town, if most of your life has been in the big city, or to be comfortable in a city of millions when your former experience has been in small towns.

The culture of the company itself is yet another environmental factor. Can an employee survive in a pressure-cooker workplace? Or will the person be able to fit in with a highly creative and interactive work group? These working characteristics are additional factors that help to define critical skills necessary for success on a job.

Thus, as we analyze the definition of the first concept, "Every job has critical skills for success," we must look first at the standard job duties. Then we must also look at the environment in which the job is performed, when we consider skills. Additionally, we must sort through what might be hundreds of specific contributing skills, and distill our list to those few that are vital. Filter the critical few from the necessary many. Focus on the make-or-break skills for success to assure long-term success. A CEO who can not build a strategic plan would not be your first pick. A janitor who never gets to work on time would not be your first pick. A surgeon who faints at the sight of blood would not be your first pick.

We've emphasized that no matter what the job, every particular job has a set of critical skills that are necessary to do the job well and succeed. We'll explore this further in a moment with another couple of exercises, but for now let's continue with the basic definition of the first key concept: Every job has specific skills for success. But what do we mean by "success?"

Stop! Think.

How would you define "success?"

Success: every job has critical skills for *success*. What did you decide is the way to define success?

Did you list items like: meets target objectives, plays well with others or gets promoted? A small example may help reinforce this part of the concept's definition.

Let's picture for a moment the stereotypical used car salesperson: pushy, slippery and shady, with a "great deal for you." Let's say that the salesperson actually makes the sale and you buy the car. Shortly afterwards, you find out that you bought a lemon. Was this salesperson "successful?" Why not? The person made the sale. The sales objective was met. Why might you think that this individual is not an example of a successful salesperson? How did you feel about the purchase? What do you do? Probably you want to complain to the company and you tell all your friends to stay away from that place or that person, right?

For our purposes here, a key issue is that success means long-term, consistent performance that meets the key objectives of the job. For example, a salesperson is successful if he or she consistently meets or exceeds the sales targets, **and** has repeat business because this person has developed a reputation for excellent support and service, **and** is able to demonstrate steady growth of sales or market penetration. Now that's a successful salesperson.

Being promotable is not a factor in defining current job success. Many people are happy to stay in their current job, with continuous contribution to the company and personal job satisfaction. They are competent and content. Their boss may be happy to leave them right where they are, and would gladly call them successful in their job. "The Peter Principle" was based on people being good in one job and being promoted to a level of incompetence. We are talking here about the skills in the job in question, not about the ability to be promoted to another job, or the person's interest in moving elsewhere. The focus of the definition is the specific current job, and those skills necessary to be consistently successful in meeting that job's requirements.

In other words, in addition to each job having its own set of specific critical skills, each job has its own measure of success, which generally translates to long-term, consistent performance with key job measures met and exceeded. Thus, to reiterate the general rule of our first key concept, *every* job has *critical skills* for *success*.

In fact, we will do a quick exercise now to hone your skills in generating useful lists of skills associated with particular jobs. I call this:

The two-minute drill

Get out your paper and pencil again, with a timer, clock or wristwatch.

We will spend a few minutes generating lists of key job skills for two different jobs. We will start with one job, and then discuss our lists, and then will go on to the next job, doing the same. Finally, we will make some additional general observations that will help you later in your own preparation for the job interview. These exercises will turn into real practice techniques for you, so pay attention!

Here are the rules of this exercise:

1. When you start the list for a particular job, jot down any and all skills that you feel are important for success on that job. Neatness does not count. You will be the only one looking at the list, so speed and quantity are the objectives (but these need to be real and thoughtful lists, not just anything to be written down).

2. Don't worry about right or wrong answers. This exercise is simply for you to get some experience with this task of listing skills for specific jobs. With practice, you will get better at this drill, and you will soon use it for your own interview preparation.

3. Take only two minutes to generate your list. When the clock gets to two minutes, STOP, and then count the number of skills you listed.

4. Proceed with the text of this chapter to compare your lists with the comments that I provide.

5. Do not look ahead in this chapter. Work the tasks listed here in sequence, reading the introductions to each two-minute drill, and then get set with your clock and your list. Do the task, review my comments, and then repeat the process with the next task.

Job One: *salespeople* (think about the best and worst people who have sold you anything, such as a car, computer, telephone, clothing, or whatever, and consider what were the skills that would be good examples of a *great* salesperson based on your own experiences).

ʌ **Stop! Think.**

Set your clock and *go* (generate your list now)!

After the two minutes, look at your list. Count the skills you listed.

How did you do? Was it easy or difficult to come up with salespeople skills?

The following are some possible skills that you might have had (this is not an all-inclusive list, but can serve as an example for your reference).

Note: for the exercise, you just needed to name the skills, you didn't need to put any definitions with them (I added definitions to these 19 sample critical skills just so you would have an idea of why I selected these important skills, and what I meant with each one. However, you know what you mean when you list the skill, and for now, that is enough).

- Product knowledge (to be able to share the characteristics and features of his or her product to help you, the buyer, understand the product's value).

- Putting the customer at ease (so you are comfortable staying a while with the salesperson to learn more and appreciate the product).

- Builds rapport quickly (you feel good talking to the salesperson).

- Appears honest about details (you sense that you heard the truth about this product versus alternative products).

- Likeable (listening to and talking with the person is a pleasant experience).

- Good communicator (explanations are easy to understand, you sense that you are making an informed choice as you select a product from this salesperson).

- Good listener (your own interests are understood, and the salesperson feeds back confirmation of understanding).

- Asks about customer needs, requirements, wishes and preferences (you sense that the salesperson really wants to know what you are seeking, so that he or she can help you zero in on the right purchase for you).

- Persistent (despite your hesitation to make the purchase, the salesperson does not give up, will continue adding more perspectives for you to evaluate, and will make follow-up contact until the sale is complete).

- Handles rejection (understanding that many customer contacts may be frustrating and result in no sale, a successful salesperson must learn to live with such failures and come back with spirit and a high energy level, time and again, to make the next sale).

- Remains calm under pressure (especially as the stakes get higher, for deadlines, tough competitive pressure and price negotiations; the salesperson maintains control with rational and persuasive points of view).

- Persuasive (makes strong arguments that convince).

- Problem solver, seeking customer satisfaction (finds ways to get through apparent obstacles, which may be buyer hesitancy, finding creative ways to balance pros and cons of one product versus another).

- Good negotiation skills (allows buyer to influence the outcome, but ultimately finds a middle ground that allows for purchase and profit).

- Good organization skills (able to manage lots of product data, time constraints, follow-up obligations, and contracts).

- Comfortable with on-the-road travel (if the job requires travel, this individual is okay with days away from home, friends and family).

- Does not cave in easily, and protects the company position (finds the fine-line between gaining customer acceptance without giving away the farm).

- After-sale follow-up (even after a sale is made, the person makes you feel important with after-sale concern for your satisfaction, offering help as needed).

- Good at enriching the sale with add-ons (helps you to appreciate the benefit of buying more than you intended).

How did this exercise feel? With your own experience on the receiving end of a sales person's skill, or lack of it, were you able to easily visualize skills that would be consistent with a top salesperson? How many skills did you gather in two minutes: a half-dozen, a dozen, more?

Let's try this one more time, with the same rules, and this time for an individual contributor such as an *accountant.* When we start the two-minute drill, quickly jot down all the critical skills that you think must be included for a successful accounting person.

165

Stop! Think.

Set your clock and *go* (generate your list for an accountant now)!

After the two minutes, look at your list. Count the skills you listed.

How did you do? Was it easy or difficult to come up with accountant skills?

Let's compare your list to some of these skills for success that may be included for an accounting job:

- Pays attention to detail (a slipped decimal point can mean a great difference in project analysis).

- Ability to work alone (an accountant often works long hours with nothing more than a calculator, computer and data. The normal work routine may involve devices more so than working with people).

- Ability to handle stress (heavy workloads that may often come in peaks typical of a month-end report, annual report, budgets or other big projects that demand overtime, long hours and steady focus).

- Knowledgeable about regulations (best accounting practices, legal definitions and technical specifics must be well understood and practiced).

- Able to draw conclusions from abstract data (in a maze of numbers, the ideal accountant can help others to see the main point and get to a decision).

- Analytical (good at studying an issue, viewing it from several perspectives, working various what-if scenarios, assessing risks and opportunities, quantifying variables, to come up with concrete recommendations).

- Good with computational software (whizzes through data with Excel and other software to quickly organize, evaluate and summarize data).

- Organization skills (can handle lots of data, for easy retrieval, analysis and manipulation).

- Strength of character (in the face of potentially hostile clients, such as department heads trying to get a project approved, or a CEO who wants to show higher profits, the accountant will hold the ground while explaining that the numbers do not support project approval, or that accounting regulations will not permit manipulation of the numbers just to make someone look good).

- Has a can-do attitude (has the ability, or skill, to persist, seeking alternatives and finding ways to push through technical or complex issues where most others may throw up their hands and give up).

- Able to explain complex accounting principles (to aid those who are clients, such as a higher level manager, peers or others in the organization who may not be savvy about accounting technicalities).

How did this second exercise feel? With your own experience on the receiving end of an accounting person's skill, or lack of it, were you able to easily visualize essential skills that would be consistent with a top accountant? Perhaps you have not had much exposure to accountants. Did this make the task more difficult? How many skills did you gather in two minutes: a half-dozen, a dozen, more?

One last exercise, and then we will discuss our overall discoveries a bit more.

This time, the two-minute drill will *not* deal with a specific job. Huh? Think about it, we have talked about two dissimilar jobs, such as a salesperson and an accountant. We saw that some of the skills were quite different, and some of the items in your two lists may have been the same. However, there are some common skills that can apply to almost any job. What might these be? Give yourself one last two-minute drill to list skills that could help someone be successful in just about any job.

Stop! Think.

Set your clock and *go* (generate your list now)!

After the two minutes, look at your list. Count the skills you listed.

How did you do? Was it easy or difficult to come up with skills that could apply to almost any job?

Let's compare your list to some of these items that may be included for most jobs:

- Initiative (the ability to see what is needed in the work environment and to take action to correct a deficiency or pursue an opportunity, even without the boss or anyone else telling you to do this).

- Ability to learn fast (for most people new to a job, this skill serves well, in order to more quickly integrate with the needs of the company).

- Integrity (the ability to adhere to core values such as honesty, fair play and keeping to your word, despite external pressures).

- Showing up on time (failure to do this consistently may get you fired).

- Showing up sober and without influence of drugs (again, a potential for immediate dismissal if this skill is not present).

We looked at critical skills for sales and accounting jobs, and then a few skills (or behaviors) that could apply to any job. Now let's think about what we have learned from these three exercises.

1. There are indeed critical skills that serve well for success in particular jobs. Without these skills, a person might easily fail to perform the function.

2. Sometimes some of these specific skills will apply to other jobs.

3. There are also some skills that may apply to many, if not all jobs.

4. Some skills relate to the technical requirements of the job (such as understanding accounting rules or engineering formulas, or the ability to remember product specifications and applications) and some skills relate to the environment of the job (such as working alone or working with others, or in-office work versus being able to handle a lot of travel). When you generate your lists, you can jog your thought process by considering different categories (technical, social, environmental) in order to create additional skills that might otherwise be over-looked, and could be important to success.

5. In only a couple of minutes you can quickly generate lists of skills that are critical to success, with more

items listed for familiar jobs, and fewer items for those where you have had limited exposure.

So what?

You may be thinking, "What do these three exercises mean to me?" As you will see in a moment, this process (thinking about key job skills for particular jobs) is your first step to interview preparation. Since every job has specific critical skills for success, it is important that you first take stock of what those skills are. These are the skills that the employer is seeking to find in the best candidate. Is your two-minute drill enough to generate the right list? No. But it does not take too much more work to get a list that can be what you need for your pre-interview preparations.

In only two minutes, you created a quick hit-list of key skills. Certainly, if you dedicated five or ten minutes, your list could have been twice as long or more. If you slept on the list for a night, and then did it one more time the next morning, no doubt you will discover a few new and important skills that your initial list omitted.

These 15 minutes could change your life!

Do exactly that: give the task about ten minutes your first time through, sleep on it, and give it five more minutes the next morning. That's a total of only 15 minutes, which could change your life. I will explain why, and how, as we continue with the next key concept in this chapter:

Predicting performance

Think about predicting future performance for a moment. Put yourself in the position of the hiring manager, the person who is doing the interviewing. You have several candidates, you talk to each of them, and finally you must make a decision about which one to pick. You are gambling the company's future, and perhaps your own career, on your selection based on a short review of résumés and a relatively brief period talking to several individuals. How can you best predict the future performance of the one you want?

You will pay the new employees from day-one on the job, with an expectation to keep paying them in the future. You will immediately expend resources to train them, get them up to speed on projects, company rules and regulations plus expected norms of behavior, and then hope that they provide a return on your up-front investments. All the risk is yours: you pay first, expend resources and then cross your fingers hoping that they will deliver later.

How can you increase your odds of prediction and selection? You have to be able to address this key question: what is the best predictor of future performance?

Stop! Think.

Write down what you think is the best predictor of future performance.

Well, what did you write? What do you think is the best predictor of future performance?

Past performance. The best predictor of future performance is past behavior in similar situations. This is the second concept.

Concept Two: The best predictor of future performance is past behavior.

The Las Vegas odds makers already know all about this concept. They make their living with this knowledge. When they are placing odds on whether one sports team will defeat another, or whether one horse will win the race, depending on the track conditions, weather, and the competition, what do these professional gamblers do? They look at past performance of that team, person or animal to see how well they did with similar conditions and challenges in the past.

You do this yourself when you watch a sports event. Imagine that a football game is into the final seconds, it's a tie score, and your team gets the ball. You hope your favorite player for end-game capability gets his hands on the ball, because you know that he can deliver in a high-stakes pressure situation. It may be a receiver, running back, or the place kicker, depending on field position. Assume in this example that it comes down to a field goal. You have confidence about the outcome since the place kicker on your team statistically comes through with a high percentage of success, and you would bet on the outcome accordingly. The pressure of the situation presents unique challenges that require special critical skills to succeed, and you know how your favorite player has consistently done in the past.

So why should it be any different when someone is trying to make predictions about performance on a job? It is not. In fact, for professional football players, this is their job! A recruiter or scout for the team would be making an analysis the same way that a manger for a non-sports oriented company would: define the critical skills for success, and find the person who has demonstrated success with these skills in the past.

If the coach needs a precise field goal kicker who handles stress well, look for those place kickers who repeatedly save the day for their team. Similarly, if the coach needs a good quarterback, running back or lineman, check the statistics of the candidate's history in those positions. The football squad also has "special teams" just for particular challenges, not unlike a company that has certain departments that specialize in unique demands for the business.

In the business world (or to say in non-sports businesses), if candidates for jobs will be required to successfully use a key job skill in the future, the best measure of their likelihood to be able to do what is needed is their historical performance. They need to show that in the past they have already had success with that skill in similar circumstances.

For example, if you need someone who can handle a crisis with calm yet decisive action (such as a firefighter or emergency rescue person, or perhaps a public relations person, or a crisis hot-line telephone person), then find out about your candidate's experience dealing with a crisis, and successfully handling incidents with calm demeanor and decisive action. Find out about multiple similar experiences, to explore this person's consistency of successful performance under these conditions.

Similarly, if you want someone to be comfortable and successful making public speeches, including being good on his or her feet answering tough questions, then find someone who has a proven track record of giving effective speeches, with apparent command and control, including interaction with a sometimes hostile public. If you were the supervisor, looking to fill jobs that demanded particular critical skills for success, then you must find the person who has most consistently, and most successfully, demonstrated these particular critical skills in the past.

The other side of the coin

The previous commentary was from the standpoint of the interviewer, trying to reduce the risk of a bad selection process by thoroughly investigating the past performance of various candidates in situations that most closely resemble the challenges the candidate will face in the new job. However, we can look at this issue from the other side of the coin, where you are the one seeking employment, rather than the hiring manager seeking a candidate.

Thus, if instead you are the person looking to win the job interview competition, in order to get the job offer, then you must approach the issue from this perspective. The supervisor wants to know about past performance with key skills, and from your point of view your task is to effectively communicate to the interviewer that you have already successfully handled the skills they are seeking. You know what they will be looking for, and you provide the data to help them make the right decision, that is to say, to hire you. You must show them that you are the most qualified person with the skills they want.

Accordingly, your first preparatory exercise, before taking an interview (actually before writing your résumé, which we will cover in a later chapter), is to prioritize a short-list of key job skills for success in the job you hope to get. By short, I mean about 10 or 15 specific critical job skills, plus 4 to 6 generic skills that apply to all jobs. If you don't know what the hiring manager is looking for, then you are not yet ready to prepare your pre-interview strategy. However, if you do the exercise we practiced earlier, you will greatly increase your own odds by anticipating what skills they will want most, and assess your own life experiences where you successfully utilized these skills.

Start with your brainstorm exercise to generate the list of critical skills (15 minutes spread out over two days). Done well, you can probably generate 50 to 75 key skills. Now prioritize them into a list that you think represents the most important ones. You need not prioritize all 50 or more items, but at least be sure you know which are the top one to two dozen skills for success for that job.

Now that you have your hit-list of key skills, the top one to two dozen that will be of interest to the interviewer (or interviewers), the objective is to communicate well about your own experiences with each of these skills in your past. You may have all the right experience, but if you cannot express your message clearly, the interviewer will not appreciate what you have to offer.

Typically, this is what happens when good people don't get job offers. It's the same as my secretary's doctor's son: he had good experience, but his delivery of the message at the interview failed. What a shame! But as you saw, it was easily fixed for him (he got the job after only one training session on these topics). Now you too will see how to express yourself clearly, concisely and with memorable impact, with concept number three, how to communicate.

Concept Three: How to be a STAR communicator during the interview.

As you can expect, and have probably already experienced, the heart of an interview is the part when the interviewer is asking you about your particular experiences and skills (in the next chapter, we will review in detail each of the phases of the interview, and what you must do to shine in each part). Here, during the question-and-answer phase of the interview, you want to be a STAR with your responses. You want to stand out brilliantly and uniquely within the wide field of competitors. How can you do this? Your interview success is tied directly to how you respond to questions about your skills.

First, let's talk about timing. Once presented with a question, how long do you think your answer should take to describe your skill to the interviewer?

What do you think? Five minutes? This is what many people think is needed. Most people feel that it takes about five minutes to form a well-composed response, with detail and examples to help the interviewer know your capability. Let's continue for the moment with that 5-minute pace in mind, and do a bit of math.

If an interview runs about half an hour, or at most maybe 45 minutes, the question and answer part may only be about twenty minutes, aside from other things that are covered in the meeting. If you take five minutes to communicate details about a particular skill, how many such Question-Skill examples can you share with the interviewer? The answer is four (discussing four skills, times five minutes each, equals the twenty minutes that are available).

What is the significance of this pace? This means that at the end of your interview, the hiring manager will have learned that you are good at four key skills for the job. Not hardly enough. If you instead were able to communicate an effective history using only two minutes for each skill question, the math says you can crank out 10 skills in the same twenty minutes. You will have communicated more than twice as many skills as your competitor during the same time period. The hiring manager will have learned about ten job-specific skills that you have successfully accomplished in your past, while only learning about four of them from the other candidates. What a dramatic difference you can make in your interview impression!

But how can you communicate all you want to about a key skill in only two minutes? The answer is to use an effective communication strategy, our Third Key Concept. You can be a "STAR" interviewee if you simply remember to use STAR communication techniques. STAR is a mnemonic device to help you remember what to do.

Wikipedia defines a "mnemonic device" (pronounced new-món-ik) as *"a mind memory and/or learning aid. Commonly, mnemonics are verbal – such as a very short poem or a special **word** used to help a person remember something – but may be **visual**, kinesthetic or auditory. Mnemonics rely on associations between easy-to-remember constructs which can be related back to the data that is to be remembered."*

In our case, the word STAR is our memory trigger. You can visualize a STAR in your head too, to help trigger your verbal response recall sequence. Each letter stands for a step in the process of preparing for and answering any question about your skill history. Just remember the topics Situation-Task-Action-Result for the word **STAR**. Here is what each part is supposed to cover:

Think STAR: Situation-Task-Action-Result

- **Situation:** this part of your response covers the situation that existed when you had to use the particular skill (the skill that is of interest to the interviewer), in order to solve a problem. Remember, your interviewer knows nothing about you or your history, therefore you must first *paint a picture with words*, briefly describing the conditions and environment when you had to solve a problem.

- **Task:** the particular challenge that you faced, or objective, where the skill of interest needed to be exercised, in order to solve the problem.

- **Action:** the summary of all actions you took to solve the problem, which will easily show your facility with the skill in question. This is the focus of your answer, and the part that you have to consider thoughtfully. Your preparation should include remembering all of the particular actions you took to solve a problem. How did you research the issue? Did you work overtime and weekends to study the alternatives? Did you engage others on your team to work on the solution? How did you motivate them to help?

- **Result:** this is the punch line to your story. Your result comment should be a quantifiable statement which demonstrates how well the problem was solved (can be expressed in dollars or time saved, income generated, sales volume increased, quality improved by X per cent, etc.). Note: it is important here to find *objective data,* whenever possible, rather than subjective comments. Rather than subjectively say "Sales improved" or "Productivity improved," it is more effective to have objective data and say "Sales improved by X%" or "Productivity improvements resulted in cutting time on the task by 25%, for a savings of $10,000 per year." If you don't recall this level of detail off the top of your head, you probably do have this data in your old performance reviews, and other work documents. Take the time to research these details before you set out for your interview.

Note: you can use your own mnemonic devices to help you remember items during the interview, or even as a substitute for STAR, if you feel another catch-phrase works better for you. In fact, when I taught this subject in Spanish as part of my semester-long course at Universidad Mayor in Santiago, Chile, instead of using STAR (a mnemonic that works for English speakers), I used "SER." In Spanish, the verb "ser" means, "to be." I told my students that they could "be" anything they wanted "to be," especially if they remembered "SER" when answering questions about skills during the interview. For them, I explained that **SER** stood for Situación (the situation or task), Evolución (the development/evolution of actions they took to resolve the challenge), and Resultado (the results of their actions).

A short example may be helpful here to show how to use STAR when addressing a question about a particular skill.

Let's imagine that the interviewer asked for an example of initiative, where you took actions on your own, without the prompting of your supervisor. Here might be a typical two-minute response that incorporates each of the STAR elements.

Situation: *"I was promoted to be the new plant manager of one of our company's oldest and largest sites (with over 700 employees, two unions and a non-union section). Unfortunately, this plant had a reputation as the highest cost plant in our company, with a poor environmental and safety record (dozens of federally reportable incidents and injuries per year), and difficult company-union relations.*

Task: *"I was asked to make quick and dramatic changes in the culture of the plant to get safety and cost reduction under control and to improve human relations.*

Action: *"I immediately had my secretary and operations manager help me with a list of the names of all the plant employees, including the details of when each would be on his or her shift (we had a 24 hour per day operation, seven days a week). I then met and talked to each employee in the work areas, such as operations personnel in their control rooms, mechanics in the shops, service personnel out in the plant and quality control personnel in the labs. I varied my areas of the plant and times of day to visit with them, including the evening and graveyard shifts. In a short time, I had met every employee face-to-face, and continued this practice every day, to know them individually, and for each one to know me, my values, beliefs and expectations. I used this opportunity to reinforce a strong message of safety, quality and cost control, clearly communicating my passion for these priorities, as well as my absolute intolerance for less than full compliance with safety and environmental expectations. Any issues the employees surfaced received my attention and follow-up.*

Result: *"Within a year, our plant won the highest corporate award for Profit Improvement. In safety, we reduced injuries to one quarter of the prior best-ever performance, from about two injuries per month to only one every other month. Our dramatic culture change, with attention to detail, also cut environmental incidents in half and slashed SARA environmental emissions (per USA Federal Government Standards) by 25% from prior years. Company-union relationships reached new heights, with a long-term negotiated agreement that avoided a strike and eliminated the need for implementing expensive contingency plans."*

This is a thorough response, and yet takes only two minutes to communicate (if you don't believe me, read it aloud and time it). It is surprising how much you can really say in only two minutes, provided it has been well planned. You can pack a lot of information into your communication when you have thought ahead about your real-life experiences, and organize the flow into this easy to follow STAR sequence. The use of STAR as the structure to respond to a question about a particular skill enables you to provide a concise, solid description of your actual past performance.

However, you do have to have prepared in advance to make the most of this opportunity. You only get one chance per question to impress your interviewer with your past success with the skill of interest to the interviewer. So how can you best prepare? And what do you do if you feel you do not have enough on-the-job experience?

Just starting out, with little experience? No problem.

The comment I often hear from those just entering the job market, either after completing their education or after at-home responsibilities now shift to seeking employment opportunities, is that "I just don't have enough experience to include in my STAR preparations." My response: "You have 20 or more years of life-skills that can serve to show you are ready!"

The key is to focus directly on the skills needed in the specific job of interest and relate them to your own non-work life experience. Let's imagine that these might include important capabilities such as the ability to learn a new task quickly, attention to detail, managing a complex project or being an innovative problem solver. Even if you have not worked for years in a professional capacity, you probably have had to use such skills in many of the following contexts: school, social events, charity activities, personal projects, extracurricular activities, hobbies, sports and within civic or religious groups. Demonstration of the successful application of a skill is valid, whether it is for a paying job, a volunteer responsibility or a self-motivated project.

Perhaps you had to plan a multi-state vacation trip for family or friends challenged with a limited budget and not much time. Your role was to optimize locations, expenses and entertainment. This may be a productive example of your skills with innovative problem solving, project management, budget control, motivating teamwork and managing priorities. Learning new skills and achieving excellence can as easily be demonstrated with your favorite hobby, sporting achievements or passions as they can with work experiences.

When you provide the situation and context of the activity, show what you did to meet the challenge, and then offer concrete examples of how you can measure success (won the regional music contest; enjoyed a 5-state vacation in one week under budget; built a one-story house as a volunteer for Habitat for Humanity), you are providing your interviewers with a strong basis to predict your future performance with their company, using the same skills that are needed on the job.

Focus on the skills, not the context. That is to say, focus on what you learned, not where you learned it. At home or at work doesn't matter. You can prepare your STARs as well as a work-based candidate would. Use the following format to be prepared.

Your STAR cheat-sheet

In preparing for an interview, after you have done the 15-minute, two-day exercise of creating your prioritized list of a dozen or so critical skills for success in the specific job in question, you should sit down with a piece of paper that can serve as your cheat-sheet, or work sheet. Here's what you do.

Across the top of a standard 8.5" x 11" paper (or A4 international standard, 210 x 297 mm) make five column headings for

Skill   Situation   Task   Action   Result

Draw lines down the length of the page for these columns.

Then down the left margin of the page, divide the page into perhaps eight or ten rows across the full page. You can do this freehand, with pencil and paper, or you can get fancy and create a blank-form for your use with an Excel program or similar text-friendly software. You will want about ten of these blank formatted pages to start. You should end up with a bunch of boxes across each row, leaving enough space to put simple bullet points with short word triggers to jog your memory in each category. For example, in our sample question-answer above, about the skill "initiative," reading across one row, your sheet might include notes such as:

Skill box: one word – initiative.

Situation box: big old plant, 700+ employees, difficult union relations, worst in costs, poor safety-environmental.

Task box: make quick changes, culture/safety/cost/human resources.

Action box: employee names, face-to-face meetings, every shift, get to know each other, strong message E/S/$ (yes, you can use abbreviations and symbols, such as in this case for "Environmental/Safety/Cost" – this is only for you, so keep it simple!).

Result box: Profit award, injuries reduced 25% of prior record, environmental emissions cut 25%, non-strike negotiation.

Once you complete a row, you now have refreshed your memory of your experience with this particular skill, and also the main points that you will want to communicate to your interviewer when asked a question about this skill.

The preparation is a three-step process:

- First, generate a good list of likely critical skills needed for success in that job.

- Second, make yourself think about your proudest and most significant accomplishments, which used those skills, one at a time, to achieve an objective.

- Your third and final step is to fill in the boxes across a row, for each skill, including simple bullet points that jog your memory of each event. If needed, check your personal files to be sure you have good data to put into the results box. Of course, never divulge classified, proprietary or confidential information.

As you prepare the boxes, take the time to review old annual performance reports or résumés that you may have in your files, to be sure you capture the actual statistics and major actions you took to make progress in your company, and also capture the data-based results that you achieved. As mentioned earlier, it is much better to be able to prepare yourself with concrete numbers instead of simply pleasant adjectives.

For this example, it is worth the effort to research and confirm, "OSHA recordable injuries were over 30 per year when you arrived at the new job, with at least two per month, and with your efforts you were able to reduce them to no more than seven incidents in one year." This is much stronger than to just put in the results-box that "Safety improved."

Our memory may get fuzzy after time, and this is why you take the time *now* to do the research and recollection about your past, before you ever go in for the interview (in fact, before you write your résumé). Fill the boxes with key words and data, which summarize the message you plan to communicate.

One last point about the work-sheet and your interview responses, before moving on to wrap-up the detail about your preparation. Once you have your bullet points, do you try to memorize a script for each skill? No. The exercise of dusting off your memory, and researching your files, is just to refresh your recollection of special events in your personal history that can demonstrate that you have successfully used each skill to solve a problem. However, this is your life. This is not somebody else's life.

Your interview response should be no different from you casually relating a story to a friend about some event in your life, while the two of you are chatting over a coffee. You were there. You remember what happened. You know the facts to communicate. The only differences are that for this important conversation (the interview) you want to check your "Results" facts first, in order for them to be on the tip of your tongue, and you want to structure the conversation to be efficient with your time, to get all the high points out in two minutes.

The STAR structure provides the flow for you, going from situation, to task, to actions and result. In fact, once you make the chart, you may not even have to look at it again, other than a quick scan before the interview. But you have to make the chart! That process gets these life-moments engraved in your memory.

What next on the form?

After you complete one row across with a skill's details, such as initiative, what do you do next on the form? Enter a new skill on the next row? No!

You should enter the same skill at least two more times, for a minimum of at least three different examples for the same "Skill" on your worksheet. Why is this? Let me give you a real-life example of an interview that will show you what can happen when you have not fully prepared.

As background, when I had a job vacancy and was interviewing candidates, I always included *initiative* as one of the key skills that I wanted to learn about from the candidate's past. Why is this? Because as a manager, with lots to do, I did not want to have to spoon-feed my subordinates, giving them instructions every day about what they needed to do. I expected them to take initiative on the job. I wanted them to use their expertise to see what needed fixing, to go after the solutions on their own, and to seek new opportunities and make them happen. I wanted to hire a candidate with a proven record of accomplishment in successfully initiating improvements at their former workplaces.

One day I was interviewing a candidate, let's call him John, and our memorable conversation went as follows (this is the truth – this is not a made-up story):

Me: *"John, please give me an example from your past where you took initiative to solve a problem. That is to say, where you saw a need for an improvement, and without being told to do something about it by the boss or anyone else, you just went ahead and took charge of the situation and made corrective changes.*

John: *"Hmmm, that is a good question. Let me think."*

Me: *Patiently waiting for a summary of John's initiative.*

John: *Deep breathing, eyes rolling upward in thought.*

Me: *Watching John's body language (his swallowing, sweat beginning to appear on his forehead, his furrowed brow).*

John: *"Nothing is immediately coming to mind, but please give me a moment."*

Me: *Offering no help, and just waiting and watching (the clock ticked on, perhaps for a minute of silence that seemed to John, no doubt, as though it was an hour!).*

John: *"Oh yes! About two years ago..." (And John went on to tell me about something he did on his own).*

After John explained this particular example of his initiative, what do you think was the next skill question that I asked? Let's continue:

Me: *"Thanks John. Now, please give me another example of your initiative."*

John: *"Hmmm. Let me think."*

Me: *More waiting.*

John: *(finally after much squirming)* *"Gee, I guess I can't really think of another example at this time."*

At that point in the interview, I had already made up my mind: I would never hire this person in my organization! I quickly and courteously finished our interview with a few more questions and moved on to the next candidate. It was obvious that initiative was not one of John's skill sets or strengths. Or, at least he did not prepare for this interview, anticipating that this particular skill might be important, so that he could jog his memory prior to the interview with real examples of his use of this skill. In any case, for me, initiative was one of the critical skills for success, and thus John's deficiency of this skill was a deal breaker.

It is understandable that with the high stress of an interview, your mind may just lock-up. Even if you have good experiences to share, you may go blank during the interview and, per Murphy's Law, you will remember the best examples only after you leave the interview. Thus, to prevent mind-lock, and to refresh your own memory of accomplishments, it is vital that you establish this practice of pre-interview preparation by filling out your form with the columns of Skill, Situation, Task, Action and Result, and the rows of specific skills, with at least three examples for each skill.

To solidify your strategy for becoming the best candidate that they will interview, you *must* do the work. Learn easy, forget quickly. Learn hard, remember forever. Do the worksheet!

Thus, make your sheet with at least three examples of each skill, before you move on to the next key skill that is on your list for the job in question. If you have many more good examples, go ahead and write them on your sheet too. There's no harm in having extra examples on your work sheet. This way, if an interviewer asks you to give another example of this same skill, you will be ready. There is another reason that you want to have at least three examples for each skill: multiple interviewers.

It is quite common, particularly for larger corporations, that the company will ask you to meet with several people during your visit. It might be the human resources manager, then the hiring manager, a senior manager (perhaps the boss of the hiring manager) and maybe even someone at a peer level or from another department. Why is this done? Because the company wants several perspectives of each candidate. At the end of the day, after all the interviewees have left, the company participants get together and compare notes. This is where they rank the candidates and share anecdotes about how the conversations went.

Imagine what happens if several of the interviewers each ask you to provide an example of a skill, such as initiative. You come prepared with your best example, but only one. You give each of them the same example. What happens when they compare notes? The first manager may say, "This guy was great! I loved his example of initiative where he did ...." Then the next managers all say, "Hey, this is the same example he gave me. Did he only take initiative one time in his career?" Instead, you want the interview team to compare notes and discover that each has *new* information to share with each other about your skills. This reinforces even further the depth of your experience and the value you will bring to their company.

Use your preparation time well. Make yourself jot down multiple life-experiences using the skills that are critical to success in the job you are seeking, so that you are well prepared to give your two-minute STAR response with ease.

Should you refer to your work sheet at the interview?

A few pages back I asked you if you should memorize your STAR response to the skill questions, and the answer was "No." Now, let's imagine that you are in the interview, and the interviewer asks you about a particular skill. Is it okay to say the following? "Just a moment, I have a good summary right here with the key points and data from my former use of this skill." In this way you won't have to memorize anything, you can just look at your notes. What do you think?

Short answer: no! The purpose of the work sheet is for your preparation, not to be used as a memory test, and not as a use-at-the-interview document. The exercise is to organize your thoughts, to give you the time to research your files and double check statistics, well before any interview is scheduled. You certainly may (and should) take your list to the interview, to give you something to look at while you are waiting (similar to looking over your notes, before you go in to a room to take an exam).

However, once you are in the interview, these bullet points should be readily available from your preparation recall. This was your life, and the details should be easy to remember. You have researched the history, and have refreshed your memory about quantifiable results. You should not need to refer to the document again while interviewing. It would look silly to take out the form and read from it while answering a question about your own life. Once a question has been asked, just take a deep breath and think about your STAR response, then smoothly go through the STAR steps for your reply.

Work and play.

Remember also, that the skill experience need not be restricted only to work situations. At-home individuals, or early in career (or fresh out of college) youngsters, long-time out-of-work candidates, and long-time-on-one-job employees seeking a job may feel they don't have sufficient examples to prepare their forms. Wrong!

As mentioned earlier in this chapter, every application of a skill counts. If you exercised this skill as part of a volunteer group, home situation, social club, or in any other role, the demonstration of the skill still applies. Frame the situation and task well, show the details of how you used this skill to solve a difficult problem and then show the quantifiable results. A good interviewer will see that you do have this skill.

A good interviewer will also appreciate if you can show your skill as a quick learner. Your preparation work sheet should have many examples of how you learn tasks quickly. These are especially important skill examples if you have not been in the working world for a while, are new in your career, or are applying for a job in a field that is quite different from the one you are currently doing. At least you can give confidence to the interviewer that you will quickly and successfully learn the tasks needed in the job, since you can demonstrate that you have done this many times in the past with similar new tasks or new responsibilities.

More than just for skills

Your STAR work sheet can also be used to prepare for other questions you might be asked during the interview, such as "Tell me about an area where you failed, and what you learned from the experience." Your interview preparation should cover not only particular skills for success on the job, but also for potential questions that address your growth, development, challenges, or other personality characteristics. However, the same format of STAR responses can serve you well to answer these questions.

In the next chapter we will address this further, as we talk about what to expect during each phase of the interview process. The point here is to know that you can use this same sheet to bullet-point situations where you faced challenges, show what you did to survive by learning and growing from that experience, and remind yourself how things turned out. Anticipate questions, prepare, and use this form to help you.

In summary

If you have done the work, your preparation for an interview will reduce your stress about what to expect. Also, you will be armed with specific examples of skills you have mastered, with good success stories for each, so that your interviewers will see that you will be a great addition to their organization. Success at the interview is all in the preparation. Make your cheat-sheet forms, think about the specific job in question (including getting input from others more familiar with the job duties), make your list of prioritized skills, and fill out your form with multiple examples of how you successfully used each of these skills in the past.

Remember these three key concepts:

1. Every job has critical skills for success.

2. The best predictor of future performance is past behavior.

3. Communicate your experiences with STAR:

   a. Situation

   b. Task

   c. Action

   d. Result

In our next chapter, we will review the typical phases of an interview, and how you can prepare best for each part.

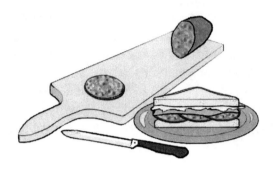

Chapter 16

<u>How to Prepare for an Interview – Part II</u>

The Parts of an Interview, and How to Prepare for Each Part

Fear

As you think about taking an important interview, do your palms get sweaty just at the thought? Does your gut begin to tighten and do your bowels begin to loosen? Sorry if I am too graphic, but this is our reality. Do you lose sleep with worry? It may not make you feel any better, but you are not alone! However, what *can* make you feel better is knowing what to do differently. You can reduce fear when you know the causes and remedies. We will address both of these in this chapter.

Your ability to reduce your anxiety before and during the interview will make a significant difference in how well you can get your message across, and how you will be perceived by the interview team. When you are fearful, your ability to concentrate on the questions asked by the interviewer may be diminished. Similarly, your ability to think on your feet, to quickly compose responses, may be riddled with mind-lock moments, where you struggle to collect your thoughts for a concise, productive description of your past experiences with critical skills. Finally, your body language may send signals of uncertainty and insecurity, both of which do not project the image you want. The key to anxiety reduction is *preparation* and *control*.

In a moment, we will discuss in detail each part of the interview process, and how you can best prepare for each phase, but let's first begin with understanding fear and how to reduce yours related to interviewing.

Control

Have you ever sat in the shotgun seat (passenger side front seat) of a car while someone else was irresponsibly (in your opinion) weaving through busy traffic? Do you find yourself pressing on the floor below your feet, as though you had a brake pedal there (or wished you did)? However, if you were in the driver's seat, you probably would not feel this sense of risk the same way, regardless of your driving style. Why is that? Let me offer one more example, before we address the possible answer.

Let's imagine we have a contest where I ask you to drive a nail deeply into a block of wood with one strong strike of a hammer, to see whether you or your competitors will best penetrate the wood. You really have to give that nail a good whack! You hold the nail perpendicular to the wood with the fingers of one hand, position the hammer above the nail with your other hand, and then draw back your arm to strike. The task may be challenging, but is not likely to generate much fear, other than perhaps the fear of not winning this hypothetical competition. However, what happens if we do the same exercise, but I ask you to hold the nail while I hold the hammer to strike?

Fear? Who holds the nail and who holds the hammer?

A big difference! All of a sudden, you feel your fingers are quite vulnerable and exposed to this high risk. Why is that?

In both examples, it is a matter of perceived control. You are never quite sure what the other person might do, either crash into another car, or smash your fingers with the hammer. If I let you hold the steering wheel of the car or hold the hammer, your sense of control and safety resume. We always feel we are safe drivers, right? We think the problem is the other half of the population who are below average (by definition) in their driving skills! Also, while we may not be the best carpenter, we still feel safer holding the hammer when we drive a nail than to have anyone else drive a nail that we hold in our fingers. Fear reduces as we sense more control of the situation.

In the interview process, many interviewees have this sense of a lack of control. They don't know what will be asked of them, they don't know what to expect of the process and they don't know how they will appear to the interviewer. Fear starts to build even before arriving at the interview location.

In reality, you have much more control than you think. First of all, the crux of the interview is about you. The interviewers are the ones who do not know who you are and what you might offer them. They are the ones who are lacking a person to do the tasks needed at the company, and they are uncertain if, or when, they will find the right person. They too have a degree of fear about the outcome, gambling their future success on unknown candidates.

With your STAR preparation, you know that you can talk with confidence about your own life. You know you can clearly communicate the message about how your experiences and skills relate to their needs. You know that with this method to deliver your key points, you will be perceived as a competent, qualified and professional candidate. You are in complete control when you are talking about your own life, especially when you have organized your thoughts about how to package these messages in bite-sized high-content STAR summaries.

In addition, you have control whenever you are talking, since you manage the pace and content of your responses. In fact, as we will discuss later, you also can control the issues themselves, based on your own questions and your own command of the discussion environment. The *wheel* or *hammer* is in your hands.

Finally, you have a great sense of control when you know what is coming. There are routine phases of any typical interview, and we will discuss what to expect when. Also, we will discuss how to be ready for each part of the interview process.

Preparation

The key to fear reduction, aside from control, is preparation. The two work hand in hand. As you understand the interview process, and prepare for each part, you will begin to feel more comfortable about yourself. You will know you are as ready as you can be, and you will have mentally rehearsed for the variety of questions that might be asked of you. This preparation will provide a greater sense of control and reduce your fear level as it frees your mind to think clearly and effectively. With your STAR worksheet preparation, you already know how you can answer the skill-related questions.

However, there are other parts of the interview, besides the skill-based questions. Thus, you need to know what each part is all about, and how you can best prepare. Let's cover that now.

The parts of the interview

How many parts are there? Think about the entire process, from the time you walk into the interviewer's office until right after you depart. What are the various phases of that process, and how many are there? The simplest answer is that there are three parts, the beginning, the middle and the end. Okay, that's a bit of an oversimplification.

I would suggest that there are five key elements within the interview process, with each having its own focus. You must anticipate the objective of each separate stage, and be ready to deliver the most favorable impression for each. They are:

1. First impressions, and breaking the ice. This could be two separate parts, but for our purposes, this phase of the interview all relates to how you are initially perceived by the interviewer, before you get into serious conversation about your skills.

2. The skills-based questions. This is the heart of the interview.

3. Your questions to the interviewer. This part of the interview may be the most often forgotten and overlooked.

4. The close or wrap-up moment of the interview.

5. The thank you note. Although officially *after* the interview itself, it is another important step in the

overall process that may be overlooked, but should not be forgotten.

Let's go through each of these five stages one at a time.

1. First Impressions and breaking the ice

You've heard the comment, "You only have one chance for a first impression." It is true, so make the most of it by knowing what is important. Consider for a moment how long it might take to generate your first impression. How long do you think? A matter of only a few minutes? That is what most participants in my seminars say, as they visualize the initial breaking the ice conversations that allow people to get to know each other.

Unfortunately, some experts say that it is a matter of seconds, from one to seven. At first, this may surprise you, but as you reflect upon your own reactions when you meet someone for the first time, you will see that this is more the norm than the exception. Probably it has to do with our species' ingrained fight-or-flight programming from a few million years ago. As animals, we all survive by quick interpretation and reaction to potential threats. No doubt, our almost instinctive sense, to look for and analyze many clues about an approaching animal or individual, allows us to feel good or threatened by the other person. We also use these brief seconds to draw many initial conclusions about them.

If this concept of quick impressions of others interests you, I suggest you read "The One-Second Personality," by Dean Bellavia, Ph.D., published by The Bio-Engineering Company. As surprising as this may seem, Dr. Bellavia describes a process for developing an accurate one-second personality analysis.

Although we may modify our first feelings as we learn more about the other person, we nonetheless form an initial impression within seconds. This all happens before a word is spoken. What then are the clues?

Body language. Accordingly, you need to think about your own body language during those initial and critically important seconds when you first approach the interviewer. During my workshops, I do simulations of a person entering an office to greet the interviewer, and then ask the audience to give feedback about what they felt about me from the body language clues that I broadcast.

Since the written format does not allow this, I will instead ask you to stop for a moment, close your eyes, and think about negative and positive body language clues that may project personality styles to the interviewer. Start with a list of negative ones. We will review those and then end with a similar set of positive ones.

Stop! Think.

Make your written or mental list of negative body language or postures.

What did you generate? Some of these characteristics may have been on your list:

- Approach to the other person is done slowly, with head down and little to no eye contact.

- The person has tentative movements, which appear uncertain or frightful.

- Eyes are darting around surroundings, or aimed downward.

- A weak handshake is offered.

- Facial expression is tense, or deadpan, with continued lack of eye contact.

- Posture in seat is closed, with arms and legs crossed, and body may be slouched or over relaxed.

- Chewing gum.

In general, the interviewer instantly receives messages from all of these physical movements displayed by the candidate entering the interview room. These postures and gestures begin to establish an impression of the person and may place the interviewee in any of the following categories by the interviewer, including people who seem to be insecure, afraid, lacking confidence, antisocial or with inappropriate behavior for the event.

For those who felt that chewing gum is appropriate, placing a higher priority on sweet breath than body posture, you would be better off if you used another form of breath freshener. You do want pleasant odors (don't overdo the perfume or after-shave either), but you can pop a breath mint in your mouth, use one of those thin-film breath strips, or use a handy pocket mouth-spray during interview breaks.

Let's do the same exercise now for more positive movements and postures. Close your eyes and visualize someone charismatic and friendly approaching you (as though you were the interviewer).

Stop! Think.

Make your written or mental list of positive body language or postures.

How did you do with this list? Are some of these items similar to ones you listed?

- Movement into the office space is done with purposeful steps, brisk and direct.

- Head is erect, back and chest are straight, and eyes are focused directly on the face and eyes of the interviewer.

- Face lights up with a sincere smile, and slight lifting of the eyebrows.

- Hand extends for a firm shake, while sustaining eye contact.

- Personal introduction is made, using name of interviewer if possible, while expressing a positive statement that is consistent with body language. For example, *"Hello Ms. Jones, my name is Artie Lynnworth, and I am happy to be here today to interview for the position of career counselor. Thank you for taking the time to see me."*

- When offered a seat, the candidate takes it with an alert posture, either with spinal column tight to the back of the chair or seated closer to the front edge of the seat with interest and intensity to the moment. The candidate avoids crossed arms and legs at first, to provide a more open look to the body.

I should mention here that these comments about the interpretation of behavior are in the context of a North American culture. In other cultures, there may be different reactions to these same *good* or *bad* postures (as defined here), so that instead of appearing friendly and in control, the approaching person may be thought to be aggressive and too forward in the context of a different culture. Instead of looking shy or reserved, this person's actions may be interpreted as respectful and proper. This is something to keep in mind if you are meeting with or interviewing with those of another culture. The point however, is that for your area, culture and circumstances, you must be aware of and consider what would be the proper message to deliver with your own first few seconds of exposure to the other person.

I've seen training instructions for interviewers which caution the interviewer to *not* categorize candidates based on their initial impressions, but to keep opinions open, waiting for data associated with actual skills. Unfortunately, this is easier said than done. It's much better for the candidate to begin with a positive impression, than to have to fight to regain credibility and admiration from an interviewer who may have hastily written off the candidate based on the first few seconds of exposure.

Assuming that you have made a pleasant first impression, with friendly, open and interested gestures, the next part of an interview's first phase is the ice-break. This is a brief period when the interviewer tries to put the candidate at ease, and to establish a bit of rapport between the two, before getting down to business with probing questions about skills and past history. As a candidate for a new job, you also need to know what to do here.

The ice-break typically will include some phrase by the interviewer such as, "Please tell me a little about yourself." This is intended to be an open-ended question, to encourage the candidate to chat for a bit. It's a way to ease into the formal interview, while initiating the data gathering process. Remember, every moment you are in the room with the interviewer is your opportunity to score points, inform, and capture interest on the part of the interviewer. There is no *off the record* moment.

One other thing to always keep in mind: the interview is always about them, the employer, not about you. Of course, the objective of the interview is to tell them all about you, but my point is that this interview is for *their* benefit. They are the ones who need to learn about you, of course, but it is their needs, their interests and their objectives that must be met.

Come to the interview with a mind-set of customer service. How can you best serve their interest, curiosity and desire? How can you reinforce that your skills are the ones that they want? You must tune in to what they are asking about, what they want to learn and what they will want from you in the future. Before you set foot into the interview office, you have to have already done your homework about the company and the job, to anticipate what key skills they may be looking for.

Accordingly, even when they ask you to "Talk about yourself," you have to do this within a context that lets them appreciate that who you are is someone they will want to have working for them. What should you cover, how long should you take and what should you emphasize?

During this ice-break, a good formula to follow related to telling your life story overview is this four-step process:

- Childhood
- Education
- Experience
- Bridge to "For this reason I am here today…"

Childhood: this should be a brief recap of you and your family roots. The key message from childhood is your value system, since that is something that lasts with you through your life, and applies to the employer, related to how you will behave in their culture. Did you come from a big family where you had to learn independence and contribute to the family activities with chores, tasks and duties? Were you an only child who learned early about doing your work before you played, and eating your meat and vegetables before you asked for dessert? What did your parents and siblings teach you about work, responsibility, honesty, respect for others and fair play? These are the kinds of quick snap-shots of your childhood that can be easily communicated and understood.

Education: what is important to the future employer? How is your schooling relevant to their work? Do your grades reflect intelligence, discipline and commitment? Were your grades a bit low, but you participated in many activities with responsibility of authority, leadership and control? Do you have the specific credentials that you know are needed to perform the tasks required by the job in question?

Experience: you will have the whole interview to discuss in detail where you worked, what you were responsible for and what contributions you made to your employers. This is not the time to rehash all of this. However, it is the time to have your sound-bite, or elevator speech ready. You have to know what your *brand message* will be when you are in the interview.

What is the basic concept you want them to retain when they think of you? It could be, for example, a solid statement of the three most important skills that they will need in the job: (1) a results-oriented, (2) fast learner, (3) dedicated to attention to detail. Whatever your message is, now is the moment to put your prior experience (professional and personal) into a boiled-down identity of who you are and what it will mean to them. This is your brand message.

A short example of this *experience* comment, with another three points, might be something such as, *"My ten years in industry have been exciting opportunities for greater responsibility, averaging a promotion and new duties about every three to four years. After entry-level technical work, I was fortunate to then become responsible first for small work teams of three to five people, until my most recent assignment as a regional manager for nearly twenty people, achieving various awards for "Best in sales," "Largest increase in year-to-year profitability," and "Highest customer service ratings" in the company. I believe my promotions were the direct result of (1) my focus on goals and results, (2) an emphasis on achieving excellence through teamwork, and (3) a philosophy of customer service (to both internal and external customers)."*

Sometimes a simple gesture, such as counting off key points 1, 2 and 3 on your fingers, as you mention them, can further reinforce your spoken message.

Simple gestures can reinforce your message.

From here, you can smoothly transition to the fourth and final re-cap comment.

Bridge to "For this reason I am here today…:" You need to let them know why you want to work for them. You can thus continue right from your experience comment to this final wrap-up message, such as, *"I've enjoyed these past ten years immensely, but my current company structure has become dead-ended, with no upward potential for growth and contribution. However, when I saw the opportunity to interview for your national manager's position, with the chance to be responsible for larger organizations, increased* *responsibility and for a company that is well known for internal growth and development opportunities, I said to myself, "This is perfect!" That is the reason I am here today."*

How long should you spend giving this life overview? About the same two-minute drill that you practiced for any of your STAR highlights. Once you outline your points for childhood, education, experience and the reason to be interviewing with them, you will easily be able to express this smoothly in a memorable and targeted way that will not exceed two minutes. Once again, this should not be memorized and sound scripted, however it should have been practiced enough by you to assure that you will make your key points for each of the four steps to "Tell them something about yourself."

This completes the first phase of the interview. Although your immediate first impression, lasting but a second or two, and then your two minutes of telling about yourself only last a few moments, this is an important part of the interview that sets the stage for all that will follow. During this introductory period, work on sustaining the proper body language, showing interest, respect, attention and friendliness. Try to use the interviewer's name at least three times during these first minutes, in order to reinforce it in your own mind, and so that the interviewer can see that you are focused on him or her. This is also a great time to take in your surroundings to get a feel for the personality of your interviewer. In fact, before going on to the question and answer part of an interview (the second step), let me first discuss this important point to help you connect with the interviewer.

Reconnaissance

While you are breaking the ice with your interviewer, try to get a sense of that person's personality and style. This is a simultaneous task, to talk, look and listen well. If you are lucky, the interview will be in his or her office, where there are many clues to their interests and personality. In fact, it also can help you in the ice-break chats. For example, as you are settling into your seat and getting started with the beginning of the interview, if you see trophies for tennis, you can notice them and remark with comments such as, "Wow, it appears as though you must be a good tennis player with all those trophies. Do you play on clay or asphalt? I have been playing doubles tennis for about ten years now, with friends twice per week, on indoor courts."

My point is to look for ways to build rapport with the interviewer, finding common ground and interests. "I love your photos of the family. You have three kids? They all look so happy together. Where was that taken? How long ago?" This should be comfortable and natural, rather than forced. So keep your eyes open and look for opportunities to connect.

Also, look for what else is in the office that can be a clue to the personality of the interviewer. Are there charts and graphs all around, showing targets and goals? Does the person have stacks of paper piled high on the desk and bookshelves? Or do you see an office with lots of family and friend memorabilia, indicating a more social, people-oriented person, rather than a data-oriented technical individual? Why does all this matter?

Simply put, people like others who are similar to them in interests and focus. Where possible, tune in to the personality of others and match your communication style accordingly. This does not mean you have to become someone else. You do not fake who you are. Instead, you are customer oriented, and deliver a message in a package that suits their interests. Let me explain.

Each of us is different. However, there are books and studies that say we all can be classified into certain broad categories. For example, one book, "Discovering Your Personality

Type," by Don Richard Riso and Russ Hudson, states that we all fit within 9 broad personality types. Another book says our behavior follows four fundamental styles. In Dr. Bellavia's book "The One-Second Personality" he groups us into what he calls Analyzer, Director, Relator or Socializer. Of course, each of us exhibits ranges within any of these behavioral classifications, often modifying our behaviors depending on the conditions, such as reverting to our natural styles when under stress or using one of our secondary styles under other situations.

Regardless of the specific categories identified in these studies or listed by these authors, you know this intuitively. Some people are detail oriented and others prefer to look at things in a more global or general way. Some people are more data oriented yet others are more social. Some are more talkative and others quiet or shy.

People with similar values and interests tend to enjoy each other's company, despite the adage that "opposites attract." I know I talk a lot, and my wife is the quiet type. We love each other very much, and we have been happily married for over 40 years. We tune in to each other's styles, and are sensitive for the clues that show interest or boredom, attention or daydreaming. Maybe that is part of what makes a successful marriage! Anyway, this attention also makes for a successful interview.

With clues in the office, and body language feedback from the interviewer, you can get a jump-start anticipating the kinds of responses that the interviewer might prefer. A data oriented person may prefer a short factual response, although a more social interviewer may enjoy a longer response that includes more anecdotal detail about situations and people associated with the topic. Even with no office clues, such as an interview conducted in a conference room, you can look for feedback clues from the interviewer.

Does the interviewer seem interested or bored, is he or she patient as you provide more details or does the interviewer seem to want to move on to the next topic or question? Look for these telltale markers and respond accordingly. Get to the point quickly with one interviewer, and embellish more with another. In any case, always keep track of your own time and control in order to maintain a pace consistent with your objective of moving through as many of your skills as you can.

2. The question and answer part of the interview

After the get-acquainted and ice-break phase of the interview, we move to the second step. This is the heart of the interview, when the interviewer is asking you questions about skills needed for success on the particular job, and you get the chance to share experiences you've had using these skills with successful outcomes. Simply, this is your time for STAR responses.

A key expression that can help you during this phase is to use the phrase "For example." This opens the door for life experiences, actions you took, results you generated. The lead-in comment "For example" will get you talking about your life, and you can use the STAR structure to get the message across effectively. If the interviewer asks you whether you have an experience you can share with him or her about your initiative, you can say, "Yes, I do. *For example*...(and then go into your STAR about initiative)."

Be sure to avoid yes-no style answers where possible, since they do not allow you to reinforce your experiences or to expand on the detail of your skills. Keep your game plan in mind related to the specific skills you want to share. If necessary, bridge to your topic, much the same as politicians do to shift from the question asked by a reporter to an answer that somehow may have only a remote connection to the topic addressed, but lets the politician pitch one of his or her themes.

This is the "answer plus one" system. Give your answer, and then add another comment that is related, and lets you make your particular point. If your strategy is to keep reinforcing your three defining skills (such as quick learner, attention to goals and results, and team focus), then keep looking for how you can get these messages out and to center stage. As always, continue to use the interviewer's name, while also maintaining your body language in a positive and attentive way.

Not every interviewer will ask the "right question." The interviewer might describe some hypothetical event and ask what you would do. That is to say, he or she may ask a question, such as "How would you handle this sort of situation?" This is actually a poor way to ask the question, from the standpoint of learning about a person's history, since the candidate can give a response that is motherhood and apple pie, filled with textbook responses of what he or she *might* do in the future. However, as we have already discussed, this will give no real information to the interviewer of what the candidate would be likely to do. The best indicator of what a candidate would probably do (as you now know) is what this person has done in the past under similar circumstances.

If an interviewer asks you this kind of question, this is still your chance to use your STAR approach. All you need to do is to begin with a transition comment such as, *"As a matter of fact, I actually had a situation quite similar to the one you described, and perhaps the best way for me to answer your question is to tell you about that real event and how I handled it successfully. For example, ..."* Always try to use your STAR response, with real past experience data, whether or not the interviewer has asked the question in the most professional way.

The Internet is full of links to questions you may be asked by interviewers. It is productive to study those questions. Sometimes they are less about skills and more about lessons. For example, interviewers may ask, "Tell me about your worst failure, what happened, and what you have learned from this." Again, STAR works for framing the situation and problem, including why it went badly, but you should also have your STAR follow-up ready. Relate to a more recent event with similar conditions where you made the right choices, learning your lesson from before, and have now mastered a proper solution with better results.

In other words, they are not picking the skill for you to address (in fact, they ask you to pick the skill), and you must be ready with your set of examples of skills that were poor in the past that are now improved or strong. As mentioned in the prior chapter, add learning experiences to your cheat-sheet preparations: include performance that went from bad to good as you matured in your role or refined your skills.

The interviewer may also probe for interpersonal relationships. You may be asked about your experiences with a difficult person and how you resolved any friction between you and the other person. However, if you think about this, the interviewer is really asking about a skill, such as resolving conflict, or building rapport, or mending fences, or creating teamwork. These are skills too. You are back to STAR for your response.

Sometimes the interviewer will hit you with something right out of the blue, that you had not anticipated during your preparations for the interview. That is okay too. Just take a deep breath. Then, restate the question in your own words to (1) assure you understand what the person wants, and (2) to buy more time as your brain is working in the background tracking through your personal history. Once you recall a situation where you dealt with this issue, go to your STAR structure to frame your answer.

Look for body language clues from your interviewer to see if you are giving too much or too little with your reply. If in doubt, too little is better than too much. The interviewer can always ask you to clarify. Too much and you bore the questioner and waste time that can otherwise be spent educating the interviewer about yet another skill.

What about salary?

The interviewer might ask you what salary you are looking for. Be careful with your answer. In general, the interview is not the time to talk salary, but instead to focus on skills. However, if you have to respond, you can first try something such as the following for your response, *"I trust your salary offer will be competitive. I am not here interviewing for a job based only on proposed pay for a first-job with your company, but rather for the opportunity to begin what I hope will be a long-term career. Also, I understand that to discuss salary alone, without taking into account the benefits, career opportunities and other non-cash issues, would be unfair to you and to me. I would prefer to continue to learn more about your company and benefits, and for you to learn more about me before we ever get into the details of specific salary offers."*

If the company wants you, they will have to provide a salary and benefit summary to you at the time an offer is made. This is when you can see if it meets your expectations, in context with all else you have learned about the company, its culture, the job, your future potential with them and any other pertinent issues for you and your family. At that point, you can negotiate, accept or decline the offer. Keep your options open as long as possible, rather than lock into a number during your first interview.

Why is it good to defer the salary discussion? Because what I addressed in the sample response above is all real and relevant. Your wages are only one element of compensation.

Benefits may account for a full third more than the straight wages or salary, when you include items such as insurance, medical coverage, prescription drugs, dental coverage, tuition reimbursement for advanced degrees, career development training, bonuses, vacation allowances, and a host of other non-cash components. Be sure you are comparing apples with apples when evaluating different job offers. It might be to your long-term advantage to take a lateral move to a similarly paying job that will give you the potential to jump a grade level or get other financial or career benefits a short time later. It is not just about up-front salary.

Secondly, as the company learns about your skills, further along in the interview process, you and they may discover that you have much more to offer them than simply filling the job for which you are interviewing. You may provide them with the opportunity to consolidate positions because you offer greater depth of skills than the typical candidate does. They can save money through job consolidation, and you can earn more for what would be an entirely different job description and pay scale. You may be able to give more dimensions to the job than their original description.

These details will only be evident to them at the *end* of the interview process, when they have all had a chance to compare notes and review their own options of how to lure you to their company and to keep you motivated with perhaps a bigger job than either you or they first anticipated.

Having said all this, if you are ultimately pressed to give a number, then give a range, in place of a single value, where your minimum is an actual pre-considered walk-away-if-not-met figure. You should have already done your homework. Find out what competitive salaries are in the market for your category of job so you already know that your range will be reasonable for the job you are seeking.

It is a waste of their time and yours if you don't have a financial floor from which you will compare all offers, and that your floor value is at least in the ball park to warrant taking an interview with this company. Know the rock bottom, but give a range, so that they and you can still negotiate based on the particular job and company needs. If you have shown your unique skills, demonstrated with your STAR communications, then your salary discussions can be more productive.

Handouts?

Yes, it is appropriate to have samples of your work (non-confidential, of course) that you may want to show them or give them. Wait for the right question, and you can pull these out of your purse or briefcase to provide a visual hook, in order to reinforce a point, and engage them in the details by touching and discussing the materials. The documents may be samples of several of your creative marketing brochures, or an article you had published. Have extras if you want to leave them with the interviewers.

Although this question-and-answer phase of the interview is the main part, and may use 80% of your total time together, at some point the interview will move to the next phase when you are asked, "Are there any questions that you have for me?"

3. Now it is your turn to ask the questions

This next phase of the interview is important, though often overlooked by candidates. You can learn a lot about the company, the job, the culture, and future opportunities by your preparation and selection of key questions for each interviewer. One of the things that often frustrated me when I interviewed candidates, and asked if they had questions for me, was when they gave me a courteous but foolish reply such as, "Thanks for asking, but I really do not have any questions for you. All of the prior interviewers did a good job of addressing all my concerns and questions, so I am all set."

Stupid! Lost opportunity! Bad impression! Why? Because this lack of asking questions gives many negative signals. Candidates giving this kind of response have lost the opportunity to demonstrate their interest and initiative, before the interview. A good candidate will have studied about the company and generated a meaningful list of real issues that need responses from those who work for the company. Particularly in my later years of work, where I was the head of divisions of the company or the general manager of an entire independent business unit, I was in a unique position to offer perspectives about the company different from any of the other interviewers on the day's schedule for the candidate.

If a candidate came to me (typically last on the sequence of interviews during the day) and said he or she already had all questions answered, my thoughts would flash along the following lines (though I would be more pleasant with any actual response to the interviewee). I would be thinking: "I don't care what the other people in my group told you, none of them can speak for me as the head of this organization. If you were smart, you would be asking me what my view of the business is, as the chief officer of this part of the company.

"You should be asking me about our competitors, the market, the projection for the next few years, my philosophy about how to run this business, how to develop people, how to do anything that would be under my direct control and influence. You could show off by explaining first that you studied the company's annual report on the Internet, before coming for the interview, and noted that there was a change in the focus during the last few years about X, and that there would be a new emphasis in areas A, B and C.

"Then you could ask me about these issues from my perspective. This would show me you do things on your own to prepare for important events. Not showing me any of this initiative tells me lots more (all bad). Only I can provide these answers. You should be jumping at the chance to get answers straight from the horse's mouth, from the head of the company, rather than be timid or lack curiosity.

"By not asking me directly, you have shown me you have missed an important opportunity, or you have demonstrated that you do not care. Neither of these impressions is favorable."

Of course, none of these words ever left my mouth. But they did run through my mind as I looked at the interviewee blankly staring back at me, who just told me "Thanks, but I have no questions for you."

Here are some examples of possible questions that a smart candidate could ask of nearly any or all of the interviewers:

- What are the main objectives of the specific job/task/department function?

- What are the most important behaviors necessary for success in this job?

- How is success measured in this job?

- How did you get to your job? What were the career experiences that made you ready when the job opportunity surfaced?

- What preparation did you do in your career to get you ready?

- How much of that preparation was by design, versus luck, to be where you were when the opportunity arose? What should I be sure to study or where should I try to gain experience for a similar job, versus what general experiences can serve me well for where I am in my career, looking to the future?

- What surprised you about your job responsibilities once you were in the job, compared to what your expectations might have been beforehand? How might I learn from this re-calibrated perspective? In other words, what might not be obvious to an outsider about what's important, and what becomes more obvious for success once you are in the job?

- What advice would you give me to best prepare for this job?

- What is a typical day like, and what skills come into play most often, or are most critical to success? Note: there are many different ways to get at the key behaviors for success on a job, and sometimes asking the question differently will get the person thinking along other lines that can be most informative to you.

- What are the prospects for advancement beyond this job? What are the key skills necessary for those next possible jobs? What does the company do to provide me with the chance to gain experience and preparation for these needed skills for advancement? How can I gain these experiences on my own?

- Why is this job vacant now? (If it's because a promotion was offered the prior holder of this position, what did that person do well that granted them the move up? If the person was fired from the job, what is it that he or she failed to do and caused the organization to look for a replacement?)

- What are the joys and satisfactions with this job? Why do you like it?

- What are the frustrations with this job, and how do you cope with them?

- What other organizations within the company are common sources of interaction? Are any particular skills needed for making these inter-group relationships more productive?

- What are the biggest challenges you face on your job? What is good preparation for being able to handle such challenges?

- How do you balance long-term vision with short-term obligations?

- What changes do you foresee in this job? Why?

- What do you want the new person to do in the first year of work on this job? What are the specific goals, objectives, and measures for results that will be used to measure the performance of the incumbent? How will you and that person know when success has been achieved?

- How does this department fit into the overall organization of the company? What are the goals of the company, and how does this job serve that objective?

- What are the department's most important projects for this year and for the next 3 to 5 years? (Is there a longer-range plan for the department and job?)

- What is the management philosophy and style related to human resources? How are people treated? How much autonomy is given to individual participants? Where on the range from micro-management to total autonomy are employees typically found, and how do supervisors differentiate between people based on their level of skill with a particular task ranging from a routine skill versus a new skill being developed?

- What can you tell me about the person who would be my immediate boss, and the others that I may have occasion to work with on a routine basis?

- How would you describe the most basic key objectives of the department and job, and what makes a great incumbent great?

You may have noticed that several questions asked the interviewer to describe the most important or critical skills for success in the job. This is the same as going to the teacher before an exam and asking what questions will be asked on the test. There is nothing wrong with asking this, and in fact, there are several advantages in doing so.

The obvious advantage is that if you ask this of the first interviewer, and you get a set of particular skills mentioned, you can attempt to include these particular skills from your past as you talk to other interviewers later in the day. The more advanced thinking time you get to reflect upon your past skills that may be of interest to the company, the more likely you will compose better STAR comments to them during the interview process.

Another advantage of asking about job skills is to compare how each manager answers your questions about these skills needed for success. If they all tell you the same key skills are critical to success in the job you are seeking, you should be impressed with how well aligned the staff is about what is important on that job and in that company.

However, if each person gives you a different list of critical skills, this disparity should give you reason to wonder if they are well coordinated, and whether they have a unified image of the company's mission, values and objectives. You can ask the same question about business strategy, goals or any other issue to see how well all the managers answer with what should be a demonstration of common focus and priority. You learn a lot about the company, its people and its culture with these kinds of questions. In addition, they continue to learn about you.

How long should you continue asking questions?

This is your opportunity to learn. Ideally, ask as many questions as you want, for the purpose to learn more about issues important to you. After all, this will become the basis for making a decision about where you plan to work. However, you do have to respect two things. One issue is the interview schedule. Are you are behind or ahead of time? The other issue is whether you are in the selling or buying mode (which I will explain in a moment).

First, let's talk about time constraints. It is common to schedule a group of candidates to do interviews the same day, each one moving through the various interviewers back-to-back. If you each are slated for a half hour interview, then the whole schedule is unbalanced if one interviewee or interviewer goes beyond the time limit. You need to be sensitive to this, and take clues from your interviewer. If the interviewer keeps looking at his or her watch, it may mean the interviewer is pressed for time and prefer that you move things along.

It is fine for you to say something like, *"I see we are running close to the half-hour scheduled for our interview, and I do not want to disrupt the allotted time. Would it be okay for me to send you a few questions later, or meet again with one of the staff members to clarify a few remaining points that I have?"* This shows respect for the interviewer's time, and your interest to have all the facts you will need to make a proper decision. Of course, don't waste time with dozens of non-critical nice-to-know details that you can get elsewhere (such as the Internet or from brochures they could give you about the company). Focus on a few key questions that show maturity and thoughtfulness, and you can leave it at that.

The issue of *buying* or *selling* will also dictate your pace with questions. During the front portion of the interview, you are selling and the interviewer is buying. What I mean by this is that at the start, you want them to buy you. You want them to hire you based on your skills and your ability to contribute. You are showing them your characteristics the same as a vendor or salesperson is trying to convince a potential buyer about the features and benefits of the product. You, and the salesperson, are working to hold interest, communicate items that catch the imagination and attention of the buyer (the employer), in order to make your sale.

However, at some point in the interview the roles may change (you hope they will), especially when the candidate begins to show the skills wanted by the employer. Look for the signs.

At one point, the employer, or interviewer, becomes the salesperson and you become the buyer. The interviewer wants you to buy the product, which is to say the interviewer wants you to work for the company. The interviewer begins to tout his or her own product's (company's) characteristics glowingly, hoping that you will be hooked with the benefits.

Look for their signs of selling. When the interviewer starts to tell you more about the company, or tempts you with descriptions of benefits, future potential, unique work challenges that you will enjoy, or offers other glowing descriptions that reflect sales talk, then you can respond accordingly. If the interviewer wants you, then the interview process will be less sensitive to the time constraints of the schedule. All of a sudden you, rather than the schedule, become the priority.

Even though this may be the case, that you see the interviewer may be willing to extend beyond the allotted time, you should be the one who is generous and courteous by asking if the deadline for the end of the interview should be honored or extended. If your host says something like, "Don't worry about the time, we want to answer all your questions," then keep learning what you can, while you continue to respect the time. Keep looking for body language signs of patience or impatience, and act accordingly.

Probably two or three key questions are enough to show you have done your homework, are interested, and care about making the right decisions. Any time for additional questions is gravy. Get what you can, but do not abuse the time of the interviewer.

Should you pull out your list of questions and refer to these?

In Part I of this section on interview preparation I asked a similar question about whether you should bring your STAR worksheet out, during the interview, as a reference guide from which you can remind yourself of key points. The answer was "No."

I ask you the same question now. When you get to the part of the interview where the interviewer asks you if you have any questions, is it all right to reach into your papers and pull out your list of questions, and refer to them? What do you think, and why?

The answer: it is okay to look at your list. Even if you just bring your list out and say something similar to the following, it can be helpful to demonstrate preparation, orderliness, interest and maturity: *"You and your staff have been excellent in addressing my concerns and questions. I don't think that I have many unanswered ones, but please let me take a quick look at the list of issues that I drafted before coming here, just to make sure."* Pull out your list (neatly typed bullet point questions that will be visible from across the desk), browse it quickly, and zero in on one or two of real interest. Watch for signals of patience and impatience, selling or buying, and behave accordingly.

Assuming that you have exhausted your list of key questions, or your time available with the interviewer, the interview will now wind down during the next and final phase. This is your last shot to leave a positive parting message. Let's review this now.

4. The close, or wrap-up part of the interview

With all else covered, your host will probably close with some courteous remarks about your interview, and a summary of what to expect next (if you have not already asked this during your question phase), such as when they might get in touch with you either way regarding the job. Finally, you have your closing comment before departing from this interviewer. This is your last chance to provide your lasting face-to-face impression, and should have the same positive impact as your first impression. What should you communicate?

Here, you should be thinking of three things:

1. Thanks (smile, handshake, eye contact).

    o   Give the interviewer a sincere comment of appreciation for his or her time and information.

    o   Remember your body language signals, to sustain eye contact while grasping the interviewer's hand with a firm shake and use of his or her name.

2. Reinforce your interest, with emotion and energy.

    o   Show that you are excited about all you have learned.

    o   Even if tired from a long day of stress and interviews, pick up your energy level to show enthusiasm, not fatigue.

    o   Be specific about something that really caught your curiosity or is a motivating characteristic of the company, such as *"I was quite interested to learn about your orientation program that lets new employees get off to a jump start with company support, so that contributions can begin right from the beginning. This is an innovative and useful approach that I have not seen in other companies."*

3. Reinforce your ability (I can do the job, I'm ready, I want to!).

   o Link the company's needs one more time with your brand message about who you are and what you bring to them.

   o Reinforce your interest in them.

   o Solidify your eagerness to contribute to the company's goals.

You always have the chance later to reject any job offer they give you, so your comments at the end of the interview are not a commitment or obligation for you to work for them. You are simply leaving them with a positive taste in their mouth about your interest in them. As the interview is progressing, from the first person to the last, keep a mental check list (or even write a list between interviewers) of items that you find are interesting, progressive, or useful, that you can use at the end of your interview during this close-out comment. Get yourself ready so that your departing words can be swift, selective and solid. Keep it simple, keep it sincere.

When you walk out the door, you are not done. Your last and final gesture to stand out from the competition is your follow-up note to each interviewer.

5. The thank you note

Within 24 hours of your visit you should send a thank you note to *each* member of the interview team that you met, *plus any others* who helped you through the day (for example if someone gave you a plant or office tour, or if an administrative assistant had arranged all the details for your travel, visit and accommodations). In the old days it might have been expected to get a postal letter by mail, but today an email done on time is better than a slow letter. Worst of all is nothing sent from you.

Anticipating that you will want to send an email, be sure to ask every person you meet for his or her business card. Not only does this help you to glance at the interviewer's name during the interview (you can keep the card open on the table top in front of you, rather than put it into your pocket), but you thus have an email address and contact information for future reference.

Use your time when you move from one interviewer to the next. While conversations are fresh on your mind, jot down notes. You may have only a few moments between interviewers, for a rest room break, or you may have to wait until the next person on the schedule is available. You can make good use of these brief pauses. Use the back of each card for this. Put a few comments there to jog your memory later with key words. It can be simple things like: *date and time of interview, tennis trophies; 3 kids; grew up in New York but went to California after Penn State. Spoke about training program for new hires.* These details will help you later to remember one interviewer from the other, after you have met a half dozen or more persons.

Your thank you note can be mostly generic in format, but be sure to leave one part personal. Even though each of the interview team may compare notes later, each one will see that at least a part of your letter was only for him or her. Your thank you can be much the same as your closing comments at the interview itself. The letter should be brief, with only a few short paragraphs. Express interest in the company, thank them for their time and education, and tell the representative that you are looking forward to hearing back from the company with a possible job offer.

In the midst of your format, mention at least one key item that was unique to your conversation with that particular person. This will remind all the interviewers of who you are (they too have seen many interviewees, all only briefly, and you need to keep reminding them of who you are and what you can bring to their company to help them achieve their goals).

Thus, with pre-interview preparation, and knowing what to expect during each of the phases of the interview process, you will be able to reduce fear, maintain a sense of control, keep your mind focused and present the best possible image to the interviewers of who you are and what contributions they may expect from you if they offer you a job with them. However, throughout all of this, remember, it is always about them!

What may surprise you is that your résumé is all about them too. How can that be? Read on to learn more!

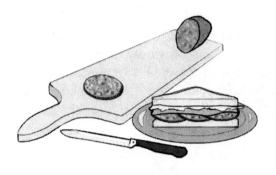

Chapter 17

<u>How to Improve Your Résumé</u>

Fundamentals first

Don't start here. If you have not yet read the two preceding chapters, on "How to Prepare for an Interview," go back and start there. It will make the task of writing a résumé much easier once you understand the basic concepts of skill-based or behavior-based screening that employers use to select the best candidates. From the foundation you will gain in those two chapters, all that follows here will be a cakewalk.

What is the purpose of a résumé?

I always begin this part of my seminars with this question, about the purpose of a résumé, because if you don't understand the objective of this document, then it is more difficult to structure it properly. What it is for dictates its design and content. Please take a moment to consider what you think is the main objective of the résumé.

Did your answer fit any of the common responses that I get during my workshops, with comments such as these?

- The purpose of a résumé is to have a concise summary of your work history.

- The résumé is prepared in order to show your various responsibilities and duties in each job you have held.

- The résumé is meant to provide not only work experiences, but also education and personal items of interest.

- The résumé includes all necessary contact information for a potential future employer.

- The résumé is a summary document whose purpose is to provide an overview of work, school and family highlights as well as major accomplishments.

Was your answer close to any of these? Do you want to change your answer? Depending on what you wrote, you may either join others who provide these typical answers, and you will be completely wrong, or maybe you will stick with what you had and you could be right. Let me explain the idea of *purpose* a bit more, and then come back to the specific reason we write a résumé and why the answers above are wrong.

Let's imagine that I stand before you with several items on top of my work bench. On the bench, you can see a board, shoe, wrench, brick, hammer, baseball bat and nail. If I said to you, "Your objective is to drive the nail into the piece of wood," what would you pick up to do the task? I suspect the nail and the hammer. Why the hammer? Because it is the most effective tool for the job. You want to drive the nail cleanly and quickly into the wood, and although any of the other items may get the job done (and although sometimes you and I may have actually used these alternatives!), the hammer is clearly designed for the task.

If I asked you, "What is the purpose of the hammer?" would you reply with responses such as these?

- A hammer is a device with a handle on one end, and on the other end a solid metal piece whose shape includes two hooks and one flat surface.

- A hammer is one of many tools in a carpenter's toolbox.

- A hammer is held in a hand to control its movement.

- A hammer may be large or small but always has a handle and head.

What is wrong with all of these definitions for describing the *purpose* of a hammer? They all explain what the hammer looks like, or how it is handled, but not what it is *for*. A hammer's purpose is to drive a nail (or with the hooks it could be used to remove one). The purpose or objective of the device is what we need to focus upon.

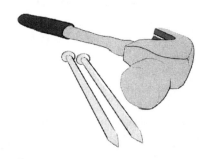

A hammer's purpose: to drive a nail. A résumé's purpose?

Thus, asking again what the *purpose* of a résumé is, we should not be describing what it looks like, or what elements compose the document, but what it is intended to accomplish. The purpose of a résumé is to achieve only one thing: *to get you to an interview*. Period.

This is the document that hooks somebody's interest. It could be the hiring manager, the human resource manager who is screening hundreds of résumés, a head-hunter (recruiter) hired to find candidates, or any other person in the process of selecting individuals for the interviews.

Thus, the tool for this job, to get you into an interview, is the résumé. Written well, it is the most effective tool for that job. There are other ways to get access to an interview. One example is a personal connection (favor) that might get you there, even without showing anyone your work history. However, you may not get much further than that step. For our purposes, we are talking about cold-contact (meaning no prior personal influence) methods to get the chance to interview. A well-written résumé is the tool to accomplish this objective.

There is a chain of command in the pre-interview screening process. For any given job vacancy, there could be dozens, hundreds or thousands of applicants, each with their best résumé, trying to get the go-ahead to come in for an interview. Normally someone is asked to do the initial screening of the bulk of résumés, such as a recruiting firm (head hunters), the human resource manager of the firm, or perhaps a delegate of the hiring manager.

From the first sorting process the bulk of applicant résumés are reduced to a manageable number for the higher ups to see. Finally, a small handful of résumés are picked for follow-up and these candidates receive an invitation to the interview. Most of the résumés do not meet the screening criteria, and only a limited few move to the next step.

Some companies will use a telephone interview to further pre-sort candidates before they invite a candidate to an on-site interview. Fortunately, the techniques discussed in the prior chapters, on how to prepare for an interview, will work for a telephone interview as well as for a face-to-face interview. Yet, you still have to grab the screener's interest to make the short-list after the phone interview. Thus, we are back to the question of how can you increase your odds to have your résumé generate the phone or in-person interview?

Make them want to meet you

The résumé has to grab their attention immediately, and keep it until they have read every word. Upon reviewing your whole document, you want them to think, "This could be the person we want!" There have to be *hooks* to keep them reading and to make you appear to be someone who has what they want.

What do they want? Well, if you learned anything from the prior two chapters, they want someone who has the critical skills for success, and a performance history that demonstrates consistent successful application of those skills in similar situations.

By now, this must sound the same as a broken record, repeating a section over and over (how many of you have even heard that sound?). Good! By now, I hope you have memorized the fundamental concepts about interviewing and matching skills with job needs. The same communication strategy that works in a face-to-face interview also works on paper. You need first to evaluate what skills are likely to be of interest to the company, and then lace your résumé with STARs.

Too often, résumés are simply a summary of job titles, job descriptions, dates and geography. You learn only about *when and where* a person had a particular title, but little about how each *contributed* to his or her company while in that responsibility. There should be less focus on a description of the jobs held, and more focus on results, contributions and the legacy you left behind.

A common mistake

Let's say as a company we are looking for a National Sales Manager. What will the likely candidate pool look like? I suspect you will guess that the majority of applicants will now be Regional Sales Managers, responsible for a large sector of the country, but not the whole nation. This is the pool of people who have already shown sales skills, have had leadership responsibility for a large area, but probably have never had overall responsibility for a whole country. They might be termed a small fish in a big pond, and now are trying to become a bigger fish.

One other group of candidates may already be responsible for national sales, but in a different field or for a smaller company (a big fish in a small pond). Both sets of candidates are essentially looking for advancement in either their own size (responsibility) or the size of the pond (larger markets), and your job vacancy seems a path to their own career fulfillment.

When I have been screening résumés for such vacancies, too often I see résumé after résumé going into too much detail describing the responsibility of a regional or national sales manager. How many different ways can you write the same thing? Moreover, I already know what these duties are. Why should I pick one candidate over another when all are essentially saying the same things about themselves? What, if anything, will capture my attention or interest? The fact of the matter is that these kinds of résumés do just about nothing to stand out. There is no *hook* for me to pick this résumé or candidate to move ahead to the next step with an interview.

However, if a few of those candidates with similar experience focus instead on the accomplishments they had while in those jobs, then that does indeed get my attention. A regional sales manager will immediately rise to the top of my short-list of candidates I want to meet face-to-face in an interview when he or she can show steady growth of markets, customer retention, market penetration, profitability, exceeding targets, and record-breaking performance.

This one change, showing contributions and achievements, can make the difference in preventing a résumé from joining a pile for no-thank-you letters, and instead allow it to join a short stack for individuals scheduled to come in for an interview. Move away from lengthy lists of job duties and descriptions and instead concentrate on skills and results.

Put in hooks and keep reeling them in one step at a time

How many of you read a newspaper cover to cover, or read an on-line version from start to finish? Probably none of you. What do we all do instead? We browse. Then, where do we stop to read? We stop at headlines that catch our interest (sports, politics, local news, science, national events or whatever)!

The style of a newspaper is a good reference guide for résumé style. It begins with a headline, lets the introductory sentence and paragraph capture the attention with a bit more detail that summarizes the main message, and then gets into more detail for those who seek the additional specifics. Your résumé should follow the same pattern. The difference, however, is that for the newspaper the reader might skip whole sections and only concentrate on one topic or article. In your case, you want the reader's attention to be captured immediately by your headlines, and then keep reading deeper into the specifics until he or she has read your whole résumé. You must catch the reader's attention and keep it for the entire résumé, leading the reader to the conclusion that he or she needs to reach you to set up an interview.

Let's work our way from the top of the page on a typical résumé, and continue down through the rest, to understand the résumé's layout and content.

Right at the top should be all the contact information the company would need to reach you. Put it first, make it clear and make it easy for them to phone or write you to schedule an interview. Be sure that your email address is professional, such as your name, and not some cute and funny expression that makes your friends laugh but is not in keeping with a business document. For example, an address such as 2beers2go@nowhere.com might get a laugh back home, but could be one more reason to toss your résumé before it ever gets off the ground.

Overview

This next section of your résumé is a great way to get your overall message out, up front, as headlines. This overview block of information is where you can summarize your career objective, with the kind of work you seek, and the general direction you hope it will follow. Then think about the top three or so most critical skills that the employer may be seeking and the most outstanding strengths that you bring to the table. If this initial headline of your key skills matches well with the company's needs, then you have a strong chance that the screeners will read on, and ultimately select you for an interview. Remember it is about them, not you. Candidates who have the skills they need are more likely to be the ones who will be selected for the interview. Always look and write from the perspective of the company's needs and interests.

If you were to label yourself, with a branding statement, as marketers do with products, what characteristics do you want to be known for? What few key skills will you repeatedly want to reinforce as you go through your interview? What performance measures always show that you excel in these abilities? This listing is the same set of key skills that you prepared in your STAR list for your first phase of your interview, when you give a thumbnail sketch about who you are. This is similar to your "elevator speech" where you succinctly state what you offer the company.

Package these traits and successes in the overview part of your résumé. Make the statements objective (using numbers) and factual. Here is where your first performance headlines go, talking about achievements such as: persistence in penetrating new markets generated a 15% increase in sales; motivation of your work team yielded a reduction in costs by 5%; creative problem solving brought a productivity increase of 13%; attention to detail brought an 8% decrease in failure rates, technical problem solving fostered an increase in quality shown by reduced scrap levels of 12%; customer focus cut complaints by 7%; passion for productivity improvement pushed an overtime reduction of 30%; and any similar summary of key skills and contributions. Whatever skill you tout, tie it to a result that directly related to the use of that skill to achieve the notable result. The overview links skills (which they want) to results (which they want too).

Body of résumé may take on one of three general forms

The balance of the résumé concentrates on your history and skills. There are normally three styles of résumés, including the chronological (the most popular), a skills-based résumé, and a combination of the two.

The chronological résumé simply begins at the top (after the overview) with the most recent work experience, and then travels back in time to the start of your career. Regardless of the years you have worked, your objective is to have the résumé take about two pages and never more than three. Any longer than that and it will probably not be read, and will be tossed into the reject pile. Boil the résumé down to essential skills and results.

If you have had many jobs of short-duration over a long period, so that it seems you need lots of space and thus several pages to detail it all, simply consolidate the history. You can say something such as "Multiple independent contractor assignments from 1995 to 2005 in the aerospace, computer and robotics industries," and then go on to detail accomplishments. A small footnote can say that you can provide more details by employer and year at their request.

In fact, you should have that ready with you at the interview (or ready to mail) in case an interviewer or recruiter asks for it. This kind of work history, without extended continuity with one employer or field, may be a reason to use the skills-based résumé instead of the chronological format.

Skills-based résumés are often ideal for those who have not shown the standard uninterrupted progression from smaller responsibility to higher duties as the date gets closer to the present. Similarly, their work history may show only short durations with any one employer. Chronological résumés allow job growth and loyalty/continuity to appear. In a chronological résumé, the résumé reviewer will see that, for example, the candidate has grown from work as a clerical sales person (such as counter sales at a department store), to local and then regional responsibility (perhaps with specific product responsibility), with positive results in each assignment (showing statistics for growth of sales volume and profits).

However, if your own history does not appear favorable in this format, or if there was a long period without work, which also would jump out in the time-format résumé, then skills-based résumés are for you. The format is driven by particular skills, and within a skill classification you can highlight various positions when and where you made your mark utilizing that skill.

The combination of chronology and skills can be accomplished by following the timing associated with your career, and within each time-cluster, stress skill-blocks to highlight examples of accomplishments. There are many Internet references to sites with helpful details for your résumé and its layout, but the key message here is to focus on skills and results, regardless of format. Hook the reader by showing you have the skills he or she needs, give sufficient objective data to support that conclusion, and entice this person to call you for an interview.

Education and Personal Data

The end of your résumé is the place to put degrees, certification and qualifications, as well as any personal data you care to include. Once again, if the message does not reinforce a skill they need, don't bother putting it there.

The potential employer may need education levels and professional certification, since these may be a requirement of the job, or such accreditation demonstrates certain skills (for example, persistence to complete a degree demonstrates long-term focus and sacrifice to meet a goal). If you have obtained special recognition, such as high class standing or other awards, these should be included here.

Personal life, aside from often being an illegal issue to address, should be limited to items that will enhance your résumé in areas not yet mentioned. For example, your volunteerism and leadership on non-work activities may increase the depth of experiences you can demonstrate for important or additional skills. Sometimes just having them in your résumé piques an interest, or offers a connection to some of the personal lives of the interviewers.

On the other hand, don't needlessly step on your own foot. You may be proud of your activities with a radical or non-popular social group, but it may generate negative reactions from those who have yet to meet you. Unless there is a direct connection to the job you are trying to get, it is normally better to omit personal items, and just stick to professional work experiences.

Triple-check for errors

There is no way to over-emphasize the importance of the basic expectation to have a letter-perfect résumé. All résumés are an immediate indication of your own pride of work, focus on detail, dedication to task, and any number of other performance characteristics that any employer will seek. Such a first impression, before they ever see you, cannot be taken lightly.

This important document is expected to have been created with great care, and double-checked by yourself, friends, family and anyone else you trust for accurate and honest feedback. The extra set of eyes is often the only way to catch a small error that you skip over as you do your own proofreading. Since you are so familiar with the work and you have read it many times, it is too easy to gloss over the detail and miss something. You need a good lumberjack on your team to see the forest for the trees. Pick a detail-oriented friend (How about that? You are using a skill assessment to select someone to do a task for you, that you know he or she has done well in the past.). Automatic spell-check software will not catch incorrect words that are spelled correctly. Get the help, and do not submit a résumé until it is letter perfect.

The quality of the résumé reflects directly on you. Just as I have benefited from the extra eyes and feedback from friends and members of my family to help me proofread this book, the final accuracy of the text rests with me. I cannot blame them for missing an error. I am the author. The responsibility is mine. This is the same with your résumé. You have final responsibility, so be sure it is error free.

Cover letters

Transmittal of your résumé is often done with a cover letter, a short focused document that refers to the attached résumé, and highlights key items for the readers. The same message applies here: stick to skills the readers want in their organization, and preview a few of your key results. This hook makes them want to read the résumé. Then follow with more hooks to encourage reading the résumé to its end.

Follow the path of skills and results to successful job offers

The résumé is your first step to a job offer. The goal of the résumé is to be invited to the interview. You need the interview to let your talent be known. The résumé, with hooks of interest to the readers, including a clear summary of skills and contributions, will gain an invitation for you to see the employer in order to provide more detail.

During the interview itself, your one goal is to get a job offer. Using your preparation of STAR communication techniques, you will leave a positive impression of your potential contributions to their organization, based on your prior success with the skills they need.

With one or more job offers in hand, you can then select the company best suited to your career interests, financial and benefit targets, long-term potential, and a culture that fits with your life style. With your end result in mind, you can successfully structure a pre-interview preparation plan and a résumé that gets you to the interview. This well planned and practiced approach can get you the job you want!

This completes the segments on pre-interview preparations, knowing what to do during each of the phases of the interview itself, as well as how to prepare your résumé to get you to the interview itself. However, before concluding with this book's slices, or tips for life and leadership, I wanted to address one concept that applies across all phases of what we have addressed so far.

That is, the consideration of ethical and value-based behaviors. In addition, we will close the book with perspectives to help your work-life balance, to seek harmony with your life's priorities. Please read on with a hearty appetite for learning just a bit more!

Chapter 18

Ethics and Values

It's all about respect

When I started this book I had a draft of chapter topics dealing with leadership concepts and tips, but I wanted to have an independent perspective from a dear friend and co-worker, Steve Kemp, whose opinion I respect. His response was immediate, "Artie, you should include one chapter about Ethics and Values." This says so much about Steve. He was absolutely right.

Steve and I worked together for nearly 30 years. He has been an inspiration and model for me throughout these years and beyond. His leadership skills grew with time, and so did his achievements and reputation. His career followed a natural and well-deserved path to his role at the time of this writing as corporate vice president of health, environment, safety and security for Occidental Chemical Corporation, a major international company, headquartered in Dallas, TX, with an employee and resident contract workforce of approximately 5,000 persons.

A credit to Steve's leadership, the Chemical Business Segment (OxyChem) of Occidental Petroleum Corporation

(Oxy) contributes to the parent company's stature as one of the world's safest employers. When writing this book, the company's Illness and Injury Incident rate was 0.63, which means that less than 1% of the employees were getting hurt per year.

More significantly, this statistic represents a mere fraction of the USA average, with Oxy having an impressively low 15% of the All-Industry USA rate of 4.20. In other words, if our company had one injury, then the average for others across the country would be nearly seven! Steve is not only an effective leader in helping guide his company to such outstanding global performance, but he is an ethical leader. You will soon see that the two go hand-in-hand.

Accordingly, when Steve suggested that I include Ethics and Values as a topic focus, I immediately saw the wisdom of this suggestion and agreed with its importance. In fact, much of what is expressed in this chapter is based on Steve's excellent review of his philosophies on this topic, which he presents to the company's future leaders as part of internal leadership development seminars. I thank Steve not only for his contributions to this chapter, but additionally for the role model he has provided for me and for thousands of others in our company and elsewhere. My respect for him, his ethics and values is without limit.

What are we talking about here?

How does the theme of ethics fit into a book on leadership techniques for success? As a start, review the various definitions we might find browsing the Internet when we search the word "ethics:"

- A system of moral principles.

- The rules of conduct recognized for a particular class of human actions or a particular group, culture, etc.

- Moral principles, as of an individual.

- That branch of philosophy dealing with values relating to human conduct, with respect to the rightness and wrongness of certain actions, and to the goodness and badness of the motives and ends of such actions.

As a leader, you play a key role in establishing the norms of your work group or social network. This includes basics such as obeying society's laws, sensitivity and respect for race relations, understanding gender issues, avoiding prejudice, appreciating equal employment opportunities and making honorable decisions.

Here's a great quote for you that I read years ago in Kenneth and Linda Schatz's book "Managing by Influence." The authors state, **"You can never not lead."** What does this mean?

The authors explain the phrase this way:

"Everything you do, and everything you *don't* do, has an effect. You lead by acts of *commission*, and you lead by acts of *omission*. You are always leading and influencing."

They go on to suggest that you ask yourself The Question of Influence: "What did I do (or not do) to make this happen (or not happen)?" They further remind us to "Realize that actions speak louder than words (and so does lip service)."

In other words, like it or not, once you are in a leadership role all of your behaviors are on display for your organization, your family and your community to observe. Leaders are looked up to, and serve as role models. You are always leading by example. There is never a time when you are not leading. "You can never not lead." It comes with the territory.

What may be surprising is that many who hold influential positions in their company or community have no idea that they are looked up to as leaders, or that they serve as models for behavior. They may not recognize that their actions could have such direct influence on the behaviors of others. However, once they internalize the powerful ability that they have to guide others, they must also remember that ethics and values are part of the package. It is not just about making targets, reaching quotas or beating the competition, but it is also about *how* the task is accomplished. The *means* to an end does count.

Let's use a small example. If the corporate safety policy says always wear safety glasses when in a maintenance work area, such as a shop, you must lead by example when you are in these areas. If you quickly pass through such an area without wearing your glasses, even if only to take a short-cut to go to the bathroom, your safety behavior sends a message about your commitment to company rules and regulations.

Your habit to follow rules is always on display, or the observation that you occasionally (or often) take shortcuts, contrary to established rules, is also on display. Your inappropriate behavior undermines your credibility, especially if at some future time you might chastise an employee for not following rules. Even your off-work behavior, on personal time, is observable and relevant. It's just part of the job, and part of what a true leader under-stands.

Some say that the organization will take on the personality of its top leaders. We know that organizations, similar to communities and nations, have a culture, or set of norms. These are behaviors that are thought to be normal (typical, appropriate) for the group as a whole. Some companies are more formal, others more informal, some pride themselves on their fast actions and dynamic risk taking, and others are proud of their well-planned and efficiently executed master plans. Within this broad sense of style or culture, there is a foundation of values, which determine what is considered the proper way to perform a job at that company.

Ethics is the foundation of leadership

It is not surprising that my friend Steve includes the following three points in his pre-hire explanation of his expectations when he interviews candidates wishing to join his department:

- Provide value and service to our customers.
  - o This is the basic theme of doing the tasks and duties well for your particular job, executing the critical skills successfully, with focus on customer service and value to the company.

- Have fun doing what you are doing.
  - o You need to be passionate about your work, to enjoy getting up every day to do what you are paid to do; otherwise, you should find something else to do.

- Conduct yourself in an ethical manner.
  - o This is the core of Steve's expectations, which leads to teamwork, credibility, providing shareholder value, and supports the conscience of the company.

Steve visualizes the relationship between effective leadership and ethics with the use of the triangle diagram, shown below. At the bottom of the figure is the foundation of honesty and integrity, which generates credibility and trust, and is the base for company leadership. At the top of the triangle is results, that is, what the company hopes to accomplish. Let's talk about what comes between these two ends of the triangle.

His concept is that if you were building a company from the ground up, you and other honest and credible leaders would begin with your philosophy of how you want to run the company, based on your theory of management principles, and visions for the organization. All is built on honesty and integrity. From this basis, you could then develop your vision statements and policies. Finally, the detail for an effective organization develops further with specific procedures for how the work is to be done, in order to yield the results that you hope will support the company's mission, visions and purpose.

However, the results themselves must still conform to the fundamentals of the company. A weak corporate foundation, built on dishonesty and mistrust will likely yield results that are far from sustainable or desired. On the other hand, when the company core values are strong with regard to ethics, and this foundation is reinforced through leadership styles that demonstrate with deeds what the words commit, then solid, honorable long-lasting performance can be the outcome.

It is my strong belief that those companies built on ethical values, practiced day-to-day by leaders who demonstrate ethical behavior (and demand no less from their subordinates), will enjoy sustainable results, assuming that they have a sound business plan. However, even with a sound business plan, those companies that are built on weak ethical foundations, or let them deteriorate over time, will soon find that their results are far from expectations. Although customers, employees, communities and stakeholders are likely to rally behind ethical leaders, they may quickly disassociate themselves from unethical leaders and companies.

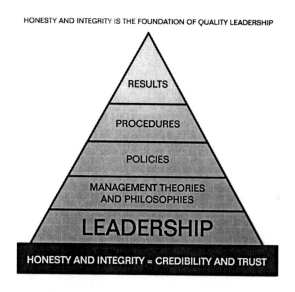

HONESTY AND INTEGRITY IS THE FOUNDATION OF QUALITY LEADERSHIP

RESULTS

PROCEDURES

POLICIES

MANAGEMENT THEORIES AND PHILOSOPHIES

LEADERSHIP

HONESTY AND INTEGRITY = CREDIBILITY AND TRUST

It is common to hear that a company's objective is to provide shareholder value. What do shareholders value, and how can you provide that? No doubt, they look for responsible operation of the business, sustainable respect for the environment, concern for stakeholders, protection of the assets, and compliance with all laws and regulations. Leaders demonstrate these values by their actions. When they and their employees embrace and practice ethical behaviors throughout the company, it is clear that their actions are consistent with their words. They practice what they preach. Organizational and individual expectations must be to practice high ethical standards.

What are your values?

Before we go deeper into the issue of leadership ethics and values with a couple of exercises, and some real-world examples of moments that test your own standards, first look carefully at the basic question about your own values and ethics. Where do they come from and how stable are they?

As we discussed in Chapter 16 about the phases of an interview and your ice-break comments regarding your childhood, I mentioned that you should talk about the influence that your parents had on the creation of your value systems. During our formative years, our parents are probably the single biggest influence on how we learn right from wrong, and how we develop a sense of behavioral norms consistent with civic responsibility and the law. We learn about respect for others, appreciating differences in gender, race and culture. We are taught about personal integrity and to not tell lies or speak ill of others.

These core values become ingrained in our internal codes of behavior, providing the conscience that in later years will guide us to appropriate behavior. Other than a significant emotional event occurring later in life, which might modify our view of life or values, it is not likely that our principles will change much from these initial foundations.

Unfortunately, some children grow up in difficult situations, where civic values, honesty and respect for others may not have been part of their formative exposures. In that case, such interviewees would be best served to address how subsequent life-lessons enabled them to develop proper core values appropriate for expected norms.

In a work environment, or in a social environment, you may find that the behavioral norms of the group in general or of individuals in particular are quite different from your own. At that point, you are likely to face conflict between your internal alarm systems and these external influences. An inner voice starts to whisper, "This is not right." The longer you tolerate this conflict, the less peace, happiness and comfort you feel in your life, job and friendships.

What you do then, after you hear the voice, starts to separate the ethical leader from the rest. Do you let your feet do the voting, by getting up and departing from the disagreeable situation at hand? Do you decide to start looking long-term for a job elsewhere? Do you talk to the others who are exhibiting what you feel is inappropriate behavior, encouraging them to get more aligned with your values? Or do you shift your own behaviors to fit in?

The following exercise may help you to better understand how you and others view potentially different behavioral styles. A bit later in the chapter, I'll provide some examples of actual situations that may serve as guides for what you can do when faced with a potential conflict.

An exercise

In your work and personal life, no doubt you have run across many kinds of individuals. Take a moment, and think about two extremes: one actual person whom you know and whom you consider a good model of ethical behaviors, and another real individual who you might consider unethical in the way he or she goes through life, on or off the job. Jot down several key words to describe each of these individuals.

Stop! Think.

Please don't just read on, but instead stop a moment, close your eyes to visualize the two individuals, and make two written lists, as you reflect on your experiences with each of them, to generate a summary of characteristics.

What did you list? Let's look first at the example you chose for the ethical person. Did some of your descriptive comments include the following?

- Honest.

- Dependable.

- Stable.

- Demonstrates strength of character.

- Unafraid to speak out against the contrary opinion or behaviors.

- This person's word is his or her bond.

- This person's actions are beyond reproach, above board and consistent with expected policies, procedures and the law.

- This person's consistent behavior generates respect for him or her as an individual.

How do you feel about him or her as a person and leader? Have you been motivated to follow this leader?

How about the non-ethical person you listed? Were any of these descriptive statements similar to yours?

- Dishonest.

- Undependable.

- Unstable.

- Exhibits weak or variable character.

- This person goes with the flow, so you never quite know where he or she really stands (this individual plays the politics of the situation, instead of demonstrating that he or she has a commitment to personal values).

- You can't count on this person to deliver what he or she says.

- This person's actions are questionable, with an undercurrent of marginal behaviors (or overtly so), contrary to required policies, procedures or the law.

- This person's behavior generates disrespect for him or her as an individual.

As you brought these people to mind, the ethical and unethical individuals, I imagine that the descriptive terms came to you rather easily. These people are quickly labeled by their behaviors. The same would be true for those who think about you. How would you be described? If those who know you made their list, in which category would they place you? The answer to that question comes from your daily and long-term behaviors, not from your speeches or lip service. Once again, keep in mind that this is the foundation of the leadership triangle, the basis from which your leadership credibility is established.

Moments of truth

"Managers do things right. Leaders do the right things" (Warren Buffet and Burt Nanus).

Day-to-day behaviors provide the backdrop of how others view leaders. This occurs through routine interactions, casual conversation or detailed work-related projects. A leader's daily consistent performance creates the basis for how he or she will be perceived. However, there are special moments, let's call them "moments of truth," when a leader's values and ethics are tested. This is the test under fire. This separates the ethical leaders from the rest. This is when they either stand firm to their values or are compromised by the pressures imposed by peers, the company culture or the situation, and they either look the other way as someone else crosses an ethical line, or they themselves step across into unethical territory.

I remember early in my career, in my first plant manager's job, receiving a phone call in my office from a product supplier. He was making a pitch for his items, knowing that I would have the final say to approve any local requisitions for purchases. Essentially, he offered a bribe. He explained that for my willingness to approve his products, I would be rewarded with a color TV (at the time this was quite a nice reward!), which would be delivered directly to my house (the implication being that no one would know). That was a moment of truth. Of course, I declined the offer, and told my purchasing manager about the incident, asking him to remove this supplier immediately from our source lists.

Later in my career, as a plant manager at the USA's largest production site of a particular product, it was brought to my attention that our process exhaust stacks *might* be way out of compliance for a particular chemical in the vent stream. I was new to the plant, and the environmental manager was taking the opportunity to advise me of a situation that before had been taboo to discuss. It made him uneasy due to the prior management's approach to the issue (the prior plant manager had abruptly departed and I was brought in).

If, in fact, the stack was out of compliance, this could mean that we might have to shut down the entire plant until a remedy was implemented, interrupting customer sales worldwide for as long as it might take to fix the problem! Another moment of truth. Do I look the other way, figuring that it was fine for my predecessor so I could follow his lead, or do I take personal action? Short story is that I immediately asked for corporate help, got experts in to review our situation, and fortunately, after thorough review of the permit conditions, sampling data and applicable laws, we clarified that we were within legal limits. I breathed a sigh of relief. At least I still had a plant to manage!

The point is that leaders will face these moments of truth, such as being offered a bribe, or learning about potential regulatory violations, when *they must make a real decision whether to hide an issue or surface it, disclose information to others or cover-up.* Never forget that during these moments, your employees, friends or family will be watching what actions you take. That is when ethics and values are tested. That is when leaders are tested. That is when your reputation is established one way or the other. That is when you get to be on people's *good list* or *bad list* as a leadership model. In addition, regardless of whether anyone is watching, these moments-of-truth decisions shape how you will live with yourself. Do you end each day knowing that you are leading an ethical life or one that shifts with blurry margins of good versus bad?

Expectations and actions

Aside from your own behavior during moments of truth, a good leader must have the courage to demand the same standards from all of the employees who report to him or her. It is not enough to go to bed each night knowing that during decisive moments you did not breach the trust of your employees nor abuse your power. You must also assure that your subordinates are following these same standards. If you find they are not, either *develop them* (train them to understand the importance of and to exhibit ethical behavior) or *ditch them* (get them out of the organization so that they do not breed destruction of the moral fiber of your organization).

Here are a couple of examples from my own experience that may provide a guide for you when facing similar moments of truth. Your critical-decision moments will no doubt have their own unique challenges. However, I hope that the following real-life situations will provide examples of how you might proceed in order to stay on the correct side of ethical leadership.

A thief on our payroll?

One time when I managed a plant, someone alerted me that he thought one of the field supervisors was getting kickbacks from a contractor. My first reaction was "No way!" This employee had a long and favorable reputation with the company, and was generally seen to be a conscientious contributor. Wow, was I surprised at this accusation.

As the site manager, with our plant located far from the corporate office, it could have been easy to just conduct a quiet little investigation on my own, with our limited internal resources, so that my plant and I would not look bad in the eyes of the company. Fear of exposing poor internal controls can be a great incentive to hide failures from upper management. Another moment of truth. I chose the more visible and ethical path.

I alerted top management and asked for assistance. With help from our corporate security department, a highly capable back-office support group, we initiated an extremely confidential investigation. Long story short, we indeed found that the supervisor was conspiring with his contractor friend. Using forensic experts and "following the money," we built a solid case of fraud. In the end, the employee was called in to my office to defend himself. After vigorously declaring innocence, he finally broke down with the truth when confronted with the unequivocal documentation we had assembled. He was immediately discharged from the company. This was beyond *developing* the employee to higher standards. This was *ditch time*.

Never lose sight of the fact that your behavior is observed by others, sometimes by just a limited few who may know you are studying a confidential issue, and at other times there may be many who never knew there was a situation until you finally take an action that becomes public. Regardless of how many see your performance on sensitive issues, your decision process and ethical behavior will support their confidence in you as a values-driven and honorable leader.

Appearances also count

A long-time public relations manager who worked for me often said, "Appearances are reality." How things appear creates the same impression as though they were real. It is more than just the act of doing something wrong that constitutes unethical leadership. The *appearance* of doing something wrong also counts.

I'll provide one last plant manager story for you, as an example of dealing with appearances. I had a human resource manager working for me, just down the hall from my corner office at the plant. Let's call him Fred. Our administrative staff was all located in the Admin Building at the front of the plant property, alongside the parking lot and adjacent to the main employee entrance. Fred was a married family man, well known in town and a long-time manager at the plant.

One day an office worker approached me in private to express concern that she thought Fred was having an affair with another of the secretaries in the office. She explained that Fred and the other secretary (let's call her Sally) were too often in private conversations behind closed doors, and it just did not seem right. I was new there, and had not yet seen any of this for myself. Nonetheless, I thanked the person for bringing this to my attention, I told her I would protect her confidential input, and explained that I would pursue the issue further myself.

My next step was to call Fred into my office to review the observation. Without saying who told me, I asked Fred whether there was any truth to the suspicion. Fred, said "No way! I am happily married, and my activities with Sally are purely professional." "Then why have all the closed door meetings?" I asked. Fred explained that Sally was responsible for employee payroll, and the two of them often had to discuss confidential issues about employees, their pay and other private matters. In our small office, Fred said that he had to protect employee confidentiality from potential eavesdropping by personnel nearby.

For me, this became a *development* moment for my HR manager. I explained to Fred that whether or not he was doing anything inappropriate with the secretary behind closed doors, the impression that there could be something inconsistent with ethical practices was dangerous to his career, his and the secretary's reputations and the company's image.

As leaders, we must assure that the organization understands and practices our standards and values. My coaching to Fred was an opportunity for me to be quite clear about my expectation of his performance. Our company's ethical standards and my own leadership values were reinforced to Fred. I wanted him to be fully aware of what was expected, and the consequences of any inappropriate performance.

As the saying goes, "where there is smoke there is fire," should be a guide for us to take action. Upon investigation, the facts may or may not substantiate the initial speculations. Nevertheless, leaders do not shy away from facing awkward or difficult situations. They must face them head-on, with confidence that the ethical approach will win-out long term.

From that day on, I kept a closer watch on Fred. Although he followed my instruction to never put himself in a closed door meeting alone with Sally, I continued to give him follow-up coaching when I saw anything else that could appear inappropriate. It seemed to me that he was still making too many visits to that particular secretary (he could as easily have just given Sally a quick phone call to discuss issues rather than walk over to her desk to chat). In my discussions with Fred, I explained that his body language, including spatial distances between individuals, continued to project an inappropriate impression. Leadership includes giving precise input and specific expectations, rather than talking in generalizations. Fred needed to know what has been, or can be observed, and what behavior is expected. He thanked me for the follow-up guidance, and assured me that there was nothing going on.

As an aside, leaders must not act just on hearsay. As issues surface, be sure to gather facts including your own personal observations in order for you to make fully informed decisions. I made one particularly enlightening observation not long after.

As I entered the parking lot early one morning, I drove right past Fred and Sally on their way into the office. Unfortunately, Fred had his arm completely around Sally's shoulder while the two of them walked together through the parking lot, as though they were lovers strolling in the park. When they looked up and saw me through the windshield of my car, Fred's face displayed instant guilt. He was caught.

Of course, I demanded he enter my office immediately. We had our own closed-door session, and he was removed from his job at our plant site that day.

I would have much preferred relaying to you a story that ended with changed behavior about appearances, but chose this one to show that it is the leader's responsibility to exhibit his or her own ethical behaviors as the leader, and to demand the same of all the members of the organization. I would hope that corrective action could be as simple as coaching unaware individuals about the impressions they leave upon others. However, if necessary, the leader has to continue observations, developing and coaching until either the person changes his or her behavior or the person is changed-out. Do not settle for less than ethical behavior.

Fred had several moments of truth opportunities. He blew each one. Each time we spoke, he could have admitted his problem, changed his behavior, and taken the ethical path as a company representative and employee. Yet, each time Fred made the incorrect decision. He covered up, rather than expose the reality. He hid the truth, rather than disclose the situation. Though it cost Fred his job at my site, it set a strong example to all the other employees that as a company we would place ethics and values where they belong: as concrete expectations of behavior to be followed without fail.

The yes-or-no test

When faced with an ethical dilemma, ask yourself the following questions to see where you stand:

- Will my actions represent legal and ethical behavior?

- Will my actions comply with the company policies and procedures?

- Will my actions comply with my company role and expectations?

- Will my actions embarrass my company, family, friends or myself?

- Do my appearances consistently conform to ethical behavior, and will they now?

You've probably seen the *embarrassment test* that you can apply, where you ask yourself, "If my actions and behavior appeared in the newspaper headlines tomorrow morning, would my parents, spouse, children or friends be shocked, and would I be embarrassed?" If the answer to that question comes up with "Yes, I would be embarrassed," or "Yes, this would shock the people who I care about," then don't do it. That becomes your moment of truth, to follow the ethical path.

One irony of this self-evaluation for decision-making is that an outright unethical person using this test probably doesn't care. Such a person may neither be embarrassed nor worry about how his or her friends react. In addition, those who know this person may not be shocked to read about him or her in the newspapers. So, when such a person faces a moment of truth, he or she might simply take the most convenient path without regard to honor, dignity or morals, and never look back. Obviously, this book is intended for a nobler sort: I hope you! The tests can guide those who are ethical, though they may be tempted to stray from time to time, and can use these tests as guides for proper behavior.

After all, how do you want to be seen as a leader, or remembered as one when you move on? In the end, all we have boils down to respect. Our ethical behavior reinforces that respect, and allows us to be effective leaders. Unethical behavior destroys respect. If at any time you forfeit the confidence and respect of your employees, you can never regain respect and esteem. They may be able to forgive, but they will never forget. Don't throw away your leadership essence.

Do you remember when in Chapter 2, "See the Flames, Smell the Smoke," we talked about effective communications? The issue of getting people to have a sense of urgency to initiate change was contingent on the ability of the leader to deliver a clear and inspiring message. We discussed the importance of removing filters from the communication channel, to improve the potential for the message to be delivered clearly, with as close to 100% of the intended topic being received by the listener. One important filter was credibility. If the listener has no respect for the person delivering the message, there is little chance that the message will be believed, or followed. The message doesn't get through the filter of disrespect. A leader must protect his or her continuous investment in building credibility and respect. Pursuit of ethical behaviors is one of the best ways to protect that investment.

Ethics, respect, leadership

We have come full circle. This entire book has been dedicated to sharing tips for leadership success. Many of the chapters were focused on a particular skill or concept. For example, "Slice the Salami," reminds you to make changes in increments. The chapter "See the Flames, Smell the Smoke," should remind you how to create a sense of urgency, with effective communications during critical situations. The section entitled "If I Only Had the Time," will help you to manage your time better. In "They Don't Wear Shoes," you had the opportunity to think about attitudes, and how they impact performance. "Visibility," reinforced the importance of knowing your people, seeing them and being seen. Finally, "The Three Eyes," image was a symbolic way to understand the progression from dreams to reality. Yet, the undercurrent through all of these chapters and tips comes back to leadership credibility.

You can make an effort to visit with your employees every day, preaching your message, but if they don't respect you, then they won't really be listening, and they won't respond in the manner you expect or desire. You can try to apply the "Four-to-One Rule," giving lots of help to others, but if you come across as insincere and only providing your help in order to position others for your own self-serving interests, you again do not succeed as a leader. You may strive to be a *change maker,* the essence of leadership, but all is lost when respect is lost. You may come up empty handed when you reach out for change.

To become the outstanding leader you hope to be, all of the leadership elements must build upon a solid foundation of ethical and value-based behavior. Your word is your bond, and your behavior is your measure of ethical stature. You must pass the moments of truth with strength and conviction, knowing it is the right thing to do. Ultimately, the rewards will be many. Leadership starts with ethics, to gain respect, to earn the leadership position you desire.

An ethics-oriented life will lead to an inner peace of knowing that you have functioned responsibly and led others by your example (you can never not lead). There are other behaviors that you can foster as well to provide tranquility, and happiness. Let's review these in the final chapter, "Be Happy!"

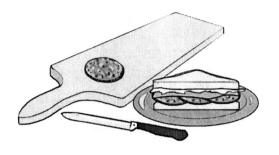

Chapter 19

Be Happy!

More than a bumper sticker

☺ Before getting started, in order to see a surprising history of the smiley face, take a look at Wikipedia's link http://en.wikipedia.org/wiki/Smiley. Who would have expected that this happy little yellow faced figure with a broad smile and two round eyes would gain such prominence in so many environments, and ultimately become adapted to computers and text message symbols as well?

One small initiative can change the world. Not that a smiley face is Nobel Prize material, but perhaps it has cheered enough people world-wide, or brought a smile to someone's face, including yours, to at least merit a moment of calm reflection. Did you just calmly reflect? Good for you. We all need to do more of that! That's the point of this final chapter. Likewise, one small change in our daily routines can change our perspective, outlook and joy.

Have fun. Be happy! ;>) Have a great day. Life is more than a dress rehearsal. Relax! These expressions and symbols, often with the omnipresent yellow smiley face, can be more than a bumper sticker statement, and can change your life. You recall the story in Chapter 13, "Discretionary Time," about the mayonnaise jar, golf balls, pebbles, sand and wine? Read it again if necessary. I love this story because of its simplicity, ease of visualization, and ultimately its powerful message. Get your priorities straight!

We sometimes rush through our days, working our checklists, jumping from one emergency to yet another hot issue, and lose sight of what may be most important: our health and loved ones. But, as the expression goes, when we are up to our butts in alligators, it is tough to remember that we were sent to drain the swamp. Take a step back, enjoy a deep breath, and reset your priority clock.

Work-life balance

For over 15 years, I have had the pleasure to work as a volunteer mentor for a worldwide company, Menttium, whose objective is to provide mid-career, high potential executives with an out-of-company mentor who can help guide their careers (see www.Menttium.com). My mentees have all been female professionals who are outstanding individuals, often with large organizations under their command, difficult business challenges and many with a near impossible dilemma of work-life balance.

I remember my own career passions and life-balance issues. On one hand, the demands of the job may dictate endless hours on-site and off-site. However, when we are passionate about what we do, it just does not feel the same as work. Most of us would not complain if we were spending long hours doing a fun hobby. If work can be fun, it doesn't feel as if it is work. The problem is that we can get sucked into a continual expansion within our 24 hours per day of dedication to that one activity, at the risk of losing touch with other facets of our life, family and friends.

I recall one leadership-training course in which the instructor talked about the benefit of getting a life outside of work.

From his comments and my own background, I came to think about this issue as a former athlete. The company's training course and my own life-lesson combined to help me understand the critical importance of two issues: priorities and rest.

When I was in elementary school in New York City, my older brother was a gymnast in high school. I began the sport early, inspired by my brother's example. I remember as a kid, watching television, and my brother and I would practice our handstands and do our push-ups in the living room during the TV commercial breaks. Our father installed a chinning bar for us, through the bedroom ceiling, supported by the attic roof above, so we could keep up with daily strength routines. Pop even provided some incentives, a penny for each additional chin-up that I could do (at the time, that was an incentive to keep exercising!). The time spent on exercises was not work. It was fun.

By the time I entered Brooklyn Technical High School, I had become hooked by the sport. Working out in the high school gymnasium and at the Brooklyn Central YMCA as well (where, by the way, Olympic gymnasts would occasionally join us), I benefited from outstanding role models for dedication, commitment to excellence and teamwork. Life-habits began to establish themselves, including persistence towards a long-term target (such as focusing on the details in order to learn a new move or to win a competition), discipline and dedication to meet goals (perfect practice makes perfect), and hard work (strength and flexibility take time and effort). By the way, are you noticing how non-work experiences can be used to reinforce *skills* needed for success?

The investment of time and effort paid off. By the time I was a senior in high school, I had been elected captain of my team and was undefeated New York City champion on the parallel bars. With advice from my older brother, when I selected a university to study electrical engineering, I picked one that also had a gymnastics team. My brother's university did not, and he said he missed being able to formally continue the sport beyond high school. For that reason, I went to Syracuse University, where another Brooklyn Tech gymnast was studying engineering and was working-out on the gymnastics team.

I enjoyed the sport there even more. In college, the caliber of competition is another level. Most Olympic gymnasts developed their skills on university teams across the country, and you can imagine the standard that our men's team had to meet. Our Eastern Region competed against Army, Navy, Penn State, University of Massachusetts, Pittsburgh, Southern Connecticut, Springfield and Temple. I used to dedicate three hours per day, six days per week to my gymnastics training, in order to build and maintain the strength, flexibility and precision of execution necessary for our competitive intercollegiate demands. I loved the sport, so it did not feel burdensome. However, I nearly flunked out of college!

I had lost sight of my priorities. My daily workouts became the priority, instead of studying to get a degree in electrical engineering, my reason for going to college. Instead of exercising my mind, I was exercising my body. It was no surprise that my first year resulted in two Ds, two Cs, and a non-credit pass in engineering orientation. I did however get an A in gym!

Of course, I needed to reset my priorities. I took a break from gymnastics. The irony is that during my first semester I did not even consider that I could cut back on my gymnastics in order to dedicate more time to studies. Kids! What do they know? I buckled-down, learned better study techniques, balanced my time and priorities better, got onto the Dean's List, got back into gymnastics, earned my Varsity Club Letter, eventually became elected captain of my university team, graduated with my electrical engineering degree, and later went on for my Masters degree in engineering administration during night school.

So when I hear about work-life balance from my mentees, I immediately think about my own college experience, as well as the training course that encouraged perspective and rest from the work routine. At the university, I had to learn priorities. Also, I know from experience, as no doubt you do too, that your muscles get tired with too much work. Even though you want to build your strength, you cannot tax the muscles 24 hours per day. They need rest. Work hard, but then rest to recuperate.

Fresh perspectives

Our minds work the same way as our muscles. They do best with rest breaks. As discussed in Chapter 13, related to discretionary time, and letting yourself rest and re-boot, how many times have you gone to bed with a problem on your mind, and have the solution when you wake up? During rest, the brain is able to come up with new answers.

During the day, it can be the same. Rather than keep pushing for the answer, sometimes it is best to walk away, take a breath, do something else, and come back to the issue later. In the meantime, the subconscious seems to address the issue with more freedom and creativity.

When I took that leadership course, the instructor mentioned that when we pursue other activities besides work, our horizons expand. In continuous learning, and especially with new hobbies, we expand our awareness of new and different subjects. What may then surprise us is that our minds can link apparently unrelated items to provide better problem-solving methods and solutions. I began to find that as my off-work time provided new experiences, other than just taking work home at night, my at-work productivity increased. I seemed to generate new and more creative solutions to my workplace challenges.

Accordingly, from my own experiences, I encourage my mentees and you to think about how you divide your day. I recommend that you set aside the time at work for forced rest-breaks, and include discretionary time in your own personal schedule. This can include the Friday afternoon 15 minutes of private time, or a daily ten-minute walk during lunch.

During your time after work, you should explore new hobbies, which means first that you leave work, and leave the work there. The inspiration of learning something new gives vitality to your life. Each new experience refines your own techniques for how to study, how to prioritize your time (so that you can enjoy the new hobby), how to learn from others (keeping your mind and body open to change), and many other skills that translate directly to work. You can connect better with others who may share similar interests, discovering new friends at work, or new alliances with co-workers and clients.

My career has allowed my wife, Margy, and me to move around the country and world, and it has also provided an automatic opportunity to reset our lives. It is almost as though we redefined who we were with our moves, our new hobbies and pastimes. Learning to fly (I received my private pilot license and flew a single engine Cessna plane for 5 years), learning to play the 5-string bluegrass banjo, learning to play classical guitar, learning a new language, doing photography, writing, traveling, practicing Tai Chi and Aikido martial arts all have enriched my life in so many ways. Find what excites you and go after it as a method to balance your priorities aside from an over-dedication to work.

Tips for life and leadership

Work can and should be fun. As my friend Steve Kemp mentioned (in Chapter 18 on "Ethics and Values"), if you don't like what you are doing at work, if you are not passionate about your professional role and contributions, then make a change. Reassess your strengths and passions, get the skills you need to excel in your preferred field, beginning with volunteer opportunities if necessary, and make a difference in your life and the lives of others. Remember my friend in New Zealand, in Chapter 7, "Continuous Learning," who felt a bit stale at work, and was evaluating major life-changes. Then we talked about how he could begin to explore new growth opportunities on the job, in preparation for whatever he might choose to do next. This became his own MBA (My Business Advancement) program of self-directed learning. It spiced up his work attitude while simultaneously helping him become ready for internal or external opportunities. If you're not having fun, think about what changes you need to make.

Life is not a dress rehearsal. You only have this one chance to contribute and to enjoy. If you want to be a leader at work or in your community, or progress within your chosen profession as an exceptional individual contributor, the best way is to be passionate about what you do. To succeed, you need to hone those critical skills for success. Yet, it won't feel as if it is work when you enjoy your pursuit of those skills through study, practice and special effort.

And life is not only about work. Life is about family, friends, faith, support to others and a host of other issues that have meaning to you. As you make a difference in the lives of others, you make a difference in your own life.

My hope is that the tips we covered in this book will provide you with a basis for evaluating how you are doing on certain issues that may facilitate your achievement of work and life goals. Manage your time better and you can fit in new hobbies and opportunities to learn new things, while simultaneously enhancing your performance on the job. Become a change maker with your own life first, and help others to change theirs. Help others and you eventually help yourself. Be ethical in all you do, and the rewards are many. Address critical issues with a sense of urgency. And for the really tough to change items in your life, remember to bite off chunks one at a time, so you don't choke. Slice the salami, and have fun in all you do.

Appendix
Another Slice for you

A cheat-sheet summary

Here's one last slice from the salami. Consider this a quick snack. Use this rapid review as a handy reference to the key points from each chapter.

Chapter 1: Slice the Salami

- Make change a slice at a time.

- Better to have a slow yes than a fast no.

Chapter 2: See the Flames, Smell the Smoke

- Sometimes you don't have time for slow change, and you must create a sense of urgency.

- Understand the communication basics of Signal, Channel, Filters, Receiver and Feedback.

- Anticipate the filters (language, credibility, distractions, etc.), and take action to improve the quality of your message's reception by the listener.

- Involve the listener to increase retention and buy-in.
- Make it personal.

Chapter 3: If I Only Had the Time

- Time Management = Planning and Making Choices.
- Link daily plans to the bigger picture (goals and life plans).
- Have a system, and stick to it faithfully.
- Review status through the day and adjust as necessary.
- Use contingency planning with the 3 Ds: Delegate, Delay and Delete.
- Distinguish between urgent versus important.
- Remember the Ferris wheel and baffle – recognize distractions and take action accordingly.
- Stay on track: Analyze, organize, leverage, monitor, re-evaluate, re-group, focus, balance, and then repeat the cycle.
- Benefit from learning systems that work for others. Get input from those you see who manage time well.
- Carve out your private time, at least once per week.

Chapter 4: They Don't Wear Shoes

- Know your attitude:
  - o If you're an optimist, double check for potential risks and downsides.
  - o If a pessimist, look for opportunities.
- Don't "Try to do it." Just "Do it!"
- Your attitude impacts others.

Chapter 5: Be a Change Maker

- Leaders are change makers.

- Start with yourself.

- Leverage leadership to amplify impact.

- People don't want to *be changed* but may indeed want to change for their own improvement

Chapter 6: The Power of Positive Reinforcement

- Consequences drive behavior.

- Negative reinforcement prompts behavior sufficient to stop the punishment.

- With positive reinforcement, discretionary effort is unlimited.

- Positive or negative reinforcement is all in the eyes of the recipient.

- Coach to success with *shaping* behavior.

- Reinforce desired behavior to avoid *extinction*.

Chapter 7: Continuous Learning

- Volunteer: it's free, practical, low risk and self-directed.

- Volunteerism can be formal (with company goals) or informal, and can be within your company, or away from work.

- Create your own MBA Program: My Business Advancement.

- To learn best, learn by doing it (hands-on activity instead of passive learning).

Chapter 8: Teamwork

- Body parts: even minor players may have important roles; value all team members.

- Participation prompts progress: engage team members.

- Moon walk: for best results, brainstorm and share perspectives.

Chapter 9: The Four-To-One Rule

- Help others four times before asking for help.

- Have a continuous *service orientation*.

- Think 360° (up, down and sideways).

- The ideal boss: track coach and high hurdles.

Chapter 10: Visibility

- Make a difference, face-to-face.

- Take stock (gap analysis), set your vision and have a clear message.

- Know your people: the difference between talking about the weather and discussing reality takes an investment in time, but it is well worth it!

- Catch them in the act (of doing things correctly), and shape behavior with positive reinforcement.

Chapter 11: Cross the Threshold

- The boss won't bite.

- "Everything you've ever wanted is on the other side of fear" (George Addair).

- Geography: near, far, near – use what works best.

- Be a sounding board for others, and use sounding boards to help your own decisions too.

Chapter 12: Don't Forget!

- My word is my bond.

- Have your process (fail-safe follow-up) and give it priority (daily commitment, updated throughout the day).

- "I will try." No! "I will."

- Verbal contracts: when you see the potential to miss a target date, give an early warning to allow adjustment of resources and priorities.

- Ask for a date rather than dictate a date (when possible), using two-step process if needed (ask for a date to give a date).

Chapter 13: Discretionary Time

- It's all about you.

- Slice the salami: pick a time (15 minutes) once per week and stick to it.

- Get your priorities straight: golf balls, pebbles, sand and two glasses of wine.

- Keep a diary of success, for personal goals and for positive self-reinforcement.

Chapter 14: The Three Eyes (I's)

- Involvement: know details and people, achieve goals, but beware of being only a bureaucrat.

- Imagination: have a vision for the future and make your plans, but be cautious of simply remaining a dreamer.

- Initiative: take action with continuous improvement to be a change maker and true leader.

Chapter 15: How to Prepare for an Interview (Part I)

- Three key concepts:
    - o Every job has critical skills for success.
    - o The best predictor of future performance is past behavior.
    - o Communicate with STAR: Situation, Task, Action, Result.
- The 2-minute and 15-minute drills:
    - o Use preparation work sheet (cheat-sheet).
    - o Minimum 3 examples for each skill.
    - o Add special situations to the preparation, such as "Your worst failure and what you learned."

Chapter 16: How to Prepare for an Interview (Part II)

- Overcome fear through awareness (know what to expect), preparation and control.

- First impressions (seconds), and telling about yourself (childhood, education, experience, and then bridge to "That is the reason I am here today.").

- Reconnaissance: tune in to the interviewer's behavioral style and adjust your comments accordingly.

- Answer questions with STARs.

- For your questions to the interviewer, be prepared. Include basics such as "What skills are needed for success?"

- Watch your time, being aware of the buy-sell atmosphere.

- Close with thanks, reinforce your interest and your ability (know your "branding" message and elevator speech).

- Provide a personal thank you note within 24-hours.

Chapter 17: How to Improve Your Résumé

- Think headlines and hooks to capture their interest to meet you in the interview.

- Focus on results and contributions rather than titles and job descriptions.

- Triple-check for errors.

Chapter 18: Ethics and Values

- It's all about respect.

- "You can never not lead." Kenneth and Linda Schatz.

- Ethics is the foundation of leadership.

- Moments of Truth: Do you stand firm to your values or are you compromised by pressure? Do you hide an issue or surface it? Do you disclose information or cover-up?

- Appearances also count.

- Use the "Yes-No Test" and the "Embarrassment Test" when you need to decide on a course to follow and when faced with an ethical dilemma.

- Ethics builds to respect which builds to leadership.

Chapter 19: Be Happy!

- Work-life balance stems from a clear view of priorities.

- Generate fresh perspectives with the use of rest and discretionary time.

- Seek your passions. If it's not fun, change!

Some good books for you to enjoy and study:

"Other People's Habits – How to use positive reinforcement to bring out the best in people around you" by Aubrey C. Daniels, ISBN 0-07-135915-X, covers the power of positive reinforcement for behavior modification.

"Managing by Influence," by Kenneth and Linda Schatz, ISBN 0-9641364-0-6, includes the quote "You can never not lead," and discusses leadership without simply exercising authority or position. To get a copy of MBI, please use this address: managingbyinfluence@gmail.com.

"Embracing Your Potential," by Terry Orlick, ISBN 0-8801-831-8, is an inspiring insight into attitude and performance.

"The One-Second Personality" by Dean Bellavia, published by The Bio-Engineering Company, offers detailed tools for quick and effective personality evaluations, and guidance on how to improve interpersonal relationships.

"Are Your Lights On? – How to figure out what the problem *really* is.", by Donald Gause and Gerald Weinberg, ISBN 0-87626-047-4, is an entertaining exploration into problem solving.

"Teaching the Elephant to Dance – Empowering Change in Your Organization," by James A. Belasco, ISBN 0-517-57478-0, Crown Publishers, Inc., is an excellent resource on how to be an organizational change maker.

"Don't Be Such A Scientist," by Randy Olson, ISBN 13:978-1-59726-563-8, provides insights on effective communication of technical information to a non-technical audience.

Acknowledgments

With heartfelt thanks to so many for helping me to create this book, I express my sincere appreciation for all that they have done.

First, to my now deceased parents, for their love, sacrifices and values they instilled in their three sons, and for their positive reinforcement to us throughout their lives, encouraging us to go after anything we wanted (i.e. to cross to the other side of fear). And for teaching us that we could be anybody we wanted to be.

To my dear wife, Margy, to whom this book is dedicated.

To my older brothers, Larry and Ray, for their early life mentoring of additional values, and for being inspiring role models of how to pursue interests with passion and dedication. In addition, for their generous willingness to read, edit and provide feedback as this book was being written.

To the publishers and authors whose works are quoted in this book, and who have given me permission to share their unique contributions to the fields of leadership, communications and human behavior.

To Steve Kemp, vice president of safety, health and environmental for Occidental Chemical Corporation, aside from his model as an outstanding and ethical leader, passionate and dedicated to his work, but also for his request to me years ago to do a corporate leadership presentation. That initiative and many of the topics in that presentation became the foundation for this book.

To John Guy LaPlante, the world's oldest Peace Corps volunteer in 2009 (at 80), author of "Around the World at 75.

Alone Dammit!" (ISBN-13: 978-0741423641), and other life experience books, for his guidance and inspiration for me to "just write." Without his mentoring and encouragement, editing and counsel, this experience, joy and book would not have happened.

To sister-in-law Bibba Spencer, for her meticulous and constructive editing, proof reading and candid feedback as this book was in its developmental and final stages. Also, for her recommendation to hire her niece, Kate Johnson, to be my graphic designer.

To Kate Johnson for the wonderful job she did to capture the fun of the ideas through her well-drawn images, while working closely with my wife, Margy, and me on the concepts and details (Reference: Kate Johnson Design, Binghamton, NY).

To Dennis Beuerle, for his detailed editorial review and recommendations that have improved the book, plus his decades of friendship, which included our college years, when his spirit and support helped me to get through.

To the members of our loving families who have enriched my life with happiness, guidance and support.

To my bosses, often my mentors, who have set examples of how a leader should perform, and how a mentor should help others. Jack Richards, my first boss after college, was the perfect model as a caring and supportive manager. He took the time to explain *why* we do things a certain way, as a patient and helpful teacher, and let me spread my wings in new roles. Paul Yoon, senior engineer, for his one-on-one technical instruction and philosophy lessons. George Kinder, for his focus on planning. Gil Parton, who took a chance on a young engineer, and let me become a superintendent in charge of dozens of field-hardened blue-collar United Steelworkers (USW) union craftsmen, and their supervisors. Jim Schutt, who showed how to give complete confidence (and responsibility) through the chain of command, working directly with his staff and expecting them to get the job done. Don Daley, who inspired with his leadership, charisma, and energy, and let me work with him to learn about strategy and planning. He moved me to new areas twice during my career, expanding my horizons and skills. Hank Antonini and Jack McIntyre, for their nurturing leadership of an electrical engineer in a chemical engineering environment. Howard Collingwood, for his "go for it" enthusiasm and risk-taking approach to make work fun and highly competitive at the same time. Pat McArthur and Hudson Smith, for their confidence in my initiatives and pursuit of challenges. Pete Piekenbrock, Joe Carona and Bob Roberson, for their manufacturing expertise and attention to detail. Les Story, for his launching me into global responsibility and high-stakes business negotiations that ultimately changed my career path forever. Ron Schuh, for enabling me to learn about making tough decisions in constructive ways. Julio Napoles, Mike Hassett and Dennis Blake, for sharing their expertise on international and corporate affairs to further develop my business and leadership skills.

To special manufacturing plant human resource managers, Susan Schanz, Paul Bowman, Mike Fatheree and Larry Ogden, for their outstanding gifts of knowing what makes people tick, how to make a team achieve unbelievable success, and how to guide me to success. Likewise, to special assistant plant managers, Roger Haley, Bert Rabbe, Bob Moore and Dave Dorko for consistent unyielding support enabling a solid team leadership effort. And to corporate international human resource managers, Ron Hamel, Chris Corwin, Geoff Seaman and Angie Thiele for their wisdom of how the executive office functions, and how to succeed in the corporate environment. Union officers Frank Marrone and Mike Rizzo for their efforts to successfully achieve teamwork in the midst of unique challenges.

To my various staffs through the years, for their spirit and support to allow us to make a difference in all that we did, helping our company, customers, community and employees. To the secretaries, administrative assistants and support personnel for their dedication to details. To the various customers who supported our businesses and provided yet another ripe field of human relations experiences. Ultimately, to all the employees who committed themselves to make change happen, setting outstanding records for safety, quality and profitability. They often provided the learning ground for me, helping me to see what works and what does not, thus the basis for all that is written here.

To the OxyChile team, in Santiago, Chile, and Talcahuano, Chile, for their patience as yet another North American general manager had to be trained in the language and culture of the country, and for their unending can-do spirit, despite some of the toughest challenges which faced our South American company in its 40-year history. Key contributors included Fernando Rubio, Carlos Muñoz, Carlos Briceño, Dave Logan, Mauricio Bruna, Manuel Castillo, and Mario Coddou (the first Chilean general manager to replace a corporate expat, and a very successful successor when I retired), Alejandra Valenzuela, Verena Moller, plus the entire Chilean organization which brought pride and success to the corporation.

To Mónica Santander Cruz, the Chilean Spanish tutor for Margy and me, and to her immediate family, who quickly became our dear friends and "family." We came to Chile the equivalent of deaf, speechless and blind. Without any knowledge of Spanish, we could neither understand the spoken work, speak the language nor read a word. Mónica brought us sight, sound and speech, and thus the ability to function as individuals and, for me, the opportunity to lead a wonderful group of highly motivated performers at work.

To Cristián Gutiérrez, our "hijo," the son we never had, for his caring, sweet and loving manner, and the joy he brings

Margy and me through his music, sincerity and intelligence. We are so proud of him and his dedication, passion and success in his chosen field.

Finally, knowing that I run the risk of omitting some key contributors to my life-experience, I want to thank a long list of specific individuals who have each played a role in shaping the direction of my own life and leadership. I would rather risk missing a few special people by oversight (I offer my apologies to you now), than to intentionally omit mentioning this host of superb individuals who each changed my life for the better.

As I write each name which follows, I have a clear and compelling reason to consider them worthy of including in this final compilation of important influences in my life: Sid Glassman, Steve Schwartz, Steve Kaplan, David Gruber, Myron Taranow, Ken Pierce, Dan Drogichen, Don Mannes, Jack Moskowitz, Chris Prestopino, Roger Maher, Roy Ratcliffe, Walt and Bethyl Dodge, Paul Romeo, Dean Bellavia, Terry Orlick, Ernie Santangelo, Ted Edwards, John and Lori Salvo, Sherry and Stewart Hesch, Charlie Huntoon, Bill Kramer, Alex Almaral, Lee Lamond, Don "Tree" Shaver, Dom Conte, Fran DiOrio, Alan Brock, Alan Levit, George Spira, Greg Lowe, John Famula, Fred Kranz, Tom Silverio, Hal Wright, Dennis Guth, Vince Lawrence, Stan Wilson, Bill Decker, Rich Palmiere, Ariff Mehter, Charlie Carberry, Gaylon and Dorothy Hoke, Nev Sachs, Ed Pluciniak, Wally Edwards, Bhaskar Bandyopadhyay, Bob Evans, Mike Puerner, Bill Baker, Marvin Miller, Gene McNeill, Ray Kirkland, Al Ford, Jim Thomson, Tom Sawyer, Stan Posey, Jim Self, Gail Hackle, Ruth Self, Anne Smith, Tom Mier, Trevor Bradbourne, Glenn Gilmer, A.J. Harrington, Bo Davis, Frank Olmstead, Rob Wolf, Jim Heppel, José Tepedino, Vern Lloyd, Clayton Jones, David Manning, Richard Lowery, David Hill, Eileen and Eddie Brunner, Norm Christensen, Robert Running, Richard Panko, Riley West, Curt and Susan Vardaro, Andy Wood,

Jule Adcock, Fred Hagan, Dwight Howell, Bob Dismukes, Sam Talarico, Candace Jaunzemis, Tom Feeney, Bob LeFevre, Bob Donahue, Bernie Carreno, Gerry Nardelli, Dave Anderson, Bill Behrendt, John Stuart, Gina Corio, Mark Rohr, Roger Corwin, Dave Bognar, Dick Maglisceau, John Maitland, Herm Harrington, Larry Fetterman, Humberto Terran, Jordan Morgan, Bill Bazell, Murray Culp, Ad Dankers, Ken Uchimura, Hiro Kamai, Shun Obokata, Rob Peterson, Don Dew, Chuck Rader, Chris Beasley, Claudia Sprowso, Marta Lopez, Fred Lietert, Michele Jacobsen, Judy Alaimo, Stacy Palmatary, Paul Williams, John Westendorf, Bill Carroll, Bob Luss, Tom Jennings, Marc Kennedy, Ken Barnhouse, Irv Kowenski, Lynn Sontag, Theresa Draper, Pat Pape, Cathy Pasquino, Elsie Chapa, Stella Lee, Gislene Martins, Fernanda Poloni, Steve Fitzgerald, Harry Schmidt, Vic Piscani, Chuck Anderson, Michael Keough, Scott King, Sergio Klaveren, Eduardo Nuñes, Helmut Metzler, Joe Hellmann, Kristin Famula, Antonia Sánchez, Roberto Smiraglia, Charles Clark, Franziskus Horn and María Elena, Francisco Muñoz and Evelyn, Antonio Yazigi, Pablo Ayala and Gina, Boris Preusser, Cristián Alvarez, Manuel Alvarez, Jaime Bazán, Fred Schiller, David Silver, Diane Greenstein, Erhard Andronoff, Cathy Casanga, Jim and Kathy Brand, Stephen Buchanan, Gonzalo Parra, Katy Cossio, Carlos Atala and Germán Senn.

Artie Lynnworth

CPSIA information can be obtained
at www.ICGtesting.com
Printed in the USA
FFOW03n0844171016
28517FF